WALKING IN THE NORTH PENNINES

Nichol's Chair - a feature of High Cup

WALKING IN THE
NORTH PENNINES

BY

PADDY DILLON

CICERONE PRESS
MILNTHORPE, CUMBRIA

Dedicated to
"T'Awd Man"

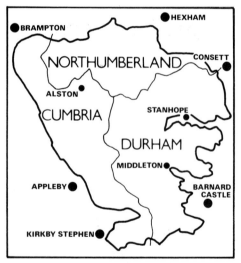

Map of the North Pennines AONB

Cover: High Cup Nick
   Photo: Walt Unsworth

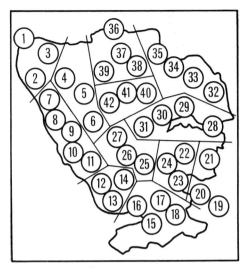

Index of Walking Routes

CONTENTS

Market Cross, Alston

INTRODUCTION

WHEN NATIONAL Parks were being established in England and Wales, the North Pennines seem to have been overlooked. John Dower described a National Park as "an extensive area of beautiful and relatively wild country". The North Pennines display the most extensive area of supreme wilderness which isn't matched on the same scale in any of the National Parks. The Hobhouse Committee recommended that twelve National Parks should be created, of which eleven subsequently achieved that status. The same committee identified other areas with great landscape value and many of these were subsequently designated as Areas of Outstanding Natural Beauty (AONBs). The North Pennines was again notably absent.

When a document recommending AONB status for the North Pennines was presented to the Secretary of State for the Environment, it was promptly filed away in a drawer to gather dust. A concerted lobby brought it back to the fore, then a public enquiry was initiated. The North Pennines became a minor battleground - "No to AONB" signs went up and some landowners declared that their property had no beauty. In June of 1988 the North Pennines was declared an Area of Outstanding Natural Beauty - the 38th such designation and at 772 square miles also the largest. There has already been a renewed call for National Park status to be granted.

The designated boundary of the AONB takes in all the high ground and most of the dales. Half of Teesdale and Weardale has been excluded, along with the major forests of Hamsterley and Slaley. Some land which is technically part of the Yorkshire Dales, but never claimed by the National Park, has been included in the AONB. This is a piece of bureaucratic nonsense - the Yorkshire Dales ends at the A66 and the North Pennines continue northwards from there. The counties of Cumbria, Durham and Northumberland administer the AONB and have jointly appointed a project officer to work there.

The Pennine Way has introduced many thousands of walkers to the North Pennines and many of them are drawn back to make further explorations. It can be confusing country - partly because of its sheer scale and wilderness quality, but also because of its access problems. Vast areas are managed for grouse-shooting, huge tracts have been claimed as strict nature reserves and the Ministry of Defence has staked out an enormous "Danger Area" subject to constant artillery bombardment.

On the plus side, there is a network of good, firm, clear tracks suitable for walking. Wilderness and lead mining are recurrent themes. Breathtaking waterfalls pour forth their glory. The flora and fauna features a bewildering host of species - some of which are unique to the area. Walkers with enquiring minds will find a wealth of interest. Forty-two day-walks and six long distance walks are offered and this is the only walking guide which tackles the whole of the North Pennines in any depth.

Geology

THE GEOLOGY of the North Pennines is basically quite simple, but it can become an exceedingly complicated study in some areas. The main bulk of exposed rocks belong to the Carboniferous Period and consists of a thickness of limestone overlain by a series of shales and sandstones which includes coal measures. The foundations underlying this succession are largely hidden and consist of ancient slates and a large area of granite.

Let's start with the bedrock, imagining a time when only the ancient slates and granite were exposed. A shallow sea lapped over that landscape and covered it with a pebbly surface. The sea was clear, warm and shallow, so corals were able to grow. As the sea deepened the corals grew ever towards the light and built up a thick reef deposit of limy materials. There were many other creatures with hard shells which lived in the sea and as these died their remains were piled up and the limy material grew thicker and thicker. Some remains were so small that the resultant limestone is very fine grained. In some cases it has simply become crystalline.

Meanwhile, much further away from this area, a vast range of mountains was being worn away by immense rivers. These rivers carried sand and mud into the sea, eventually reaching this area. The mud cut out the light and killed off the corals. Mud banks built up over the reefs. In times of severe flooding sand was carried into the sea and dumped on top of the mudbanks. This inter-bedded series eventually built up so that it occasionally stood slightly above the sea. It was in fact a vast delta system which came to cover the area. Sometimes strange fern-like trees or giant horsetail-type plants could get a roothold, but fluctuating water levels sometimes drowned the lot. The vegetable matter would become entombed in further layers of sand and mud. In time it turned into coal.

The whole series which is displayed today - limestones, shales and sandstones - is tilted back slightly from west to east. For all intents and purposes, this tilt is so slight that many small locations could be said to display horizontal strata. However, given that the tilt is over many miles, it means that limestones are more commonly exposed in the west and shales and sandstones in the east. There are also a series of fault-lines which have upset the simple succession and broken the area into separate blocks whose strata don't quite match. The arrangement is further upset by the presence of the Whin Sill - a foreign rock which arrived as a molten sheet squeezed between the existing layered succession. Incredible heat and pressures also forced hot gases and liquids into the rocks, which cooled to form mineral veins, containing metals and other substances foreign to the original series.

A geological map is an interesting accompaniment on many of the walks, enabling rock types to be identified and named. These maps, plus some detailed back-up reading, would help the walker to interpret the very complicated arrangement of foothills along the East Fellside flank of the North Pennines. A complex fault-line has mixed up the simple succession with the older bedrocks, breaking each series apart before tilting and mis-matching them. The East Fellside is a specialist study - something to look at if you want a PhD.

The Whin Sill

WHINSTONE IS simply a northern name for a hard stone. A sill is a level bed of rock, but more particularly a level bed which was once in a molten state. What distinguishes the Whin Sill from all other level beds of rock in the North Pennines is its composition and formation. In the beginning were the level beds of the Carboniferous Period - the limestones, shales and sandstones. An area of volcanic activity far from the Pennines was spewing out masses of basaltic lava on what was then the surface of the Earth. Not all the material poured out - some of it was squeezed by immense pressure between the existing layered beds of rock. This is how the Whin Sill reached the North Pennines - as a sheet of molten rock forced into the subterranean succession.

A number of things happened during the process. Some of the existing rock melted and became part of the composition of the Whin Sill. Other rocks simply baked until they were quite changed by the heat and pressure. The "Sugar Limestone" of Upper Teesdale was once an ordinary limestone until it was baked by the heat of the Whin Sill. Many of Upper Teesdale's unique plants need the particular sub-soil created by the Sugar Limestone if they are to survive, and the Sugar Limestone itself was created by the arrival of the Whin Sill. As the heat dissipated into the surrounding strata, the Whin Sill cooled, solidified and remained trapped.

Weather processes have acted on the rock succession and the Whin Sill's hardness has allowed it to stand out fairly prominently. The line of the Whin Sill can be traced all along the length of the East Fellside flank of the North Pennines and along the line of nearby Hadrian's Wall. Sometimes it only presents a slight break of slope. At other times it occurs as a fringe of boulders. In some small dales it gives rise to an impressive cliff-line. Many watercourses which run over it break into sudden waterfalls. Sometimes the waterfalls are impressive, such as Cauldron Snout, High Force and Low Force. At other times they have to be searched out, such as the small waterfalls on Croglin Fell or Cold Fell. In some areas the hard whinstone has been quarried for roadstone.

Scenery

THE GEOLOGY of an area ultimately determines the sort of landforms it can feature. The succession of shales and sandstones on the higher moors presents a series of steps where the harder strata have resisted weathering. Level beds of rock give rise to many level summit areas. Watercourses are broken into waterfalls where they encounter resistant beds. The sandstones and shales break down to form a poor soil which has encouraged the formation of acid peat moorlands. Below these beds, the limestone presents some similar features and some quite different ones. There is the same stepped appearance where harder beds of limestone prove to be weather resistant. Limestone is also slightly soluble and the water is slightly acid, so an intricate system of subterranean channels has evolved. Many streams simply disappear when they flow onto limestone, then re-emerge when they encounter a different rock type. Powerful streams can cut impressive gorges in the limestone beds and polish the rock to perfection. The occurrence of limestone below the soil is often indicated by the appearance of conical hollows, or a change from wiry moorland grass to short, green turf.

The Whin Sill provides its own particular brand of scenery, which has already been mentioned. Man's search for minerals has presented a series of disturbances to the scene and many of these are readily identifiable in the open vistas. The open vistas have been created by the removal of the once-extensive forest cover. This has encouraged the establishment of moorland vegetation, which has been developed for the sport of grouse-shooting. Man's need for food has resulted in the moorland being pushed back to 2,000 feet (600 metres) or more. Communications between dales have resulted in a network of high tracks and roads - even railways once ran to prodigious height in the region. Although the geology plays a large part in the development of landforms, man's hand has greatly altered the natural order and much of the scenery is man-managed.

Weather

THIS IS high, exposed wilderness country. Winds howl unrestrained across the moors and there is little shelter from it. Rainfall is high and the peat bogs hold considerable quantities of water. Mist is common on the high ground and navigation can be confusing as there are few landmarks in many places. Winters are hard, bringing sweeping drifts which are slow to clear. Cross Fell holds the English record for snow cover into the month of July. Even motoring can be hazardous, let alone walking. Clear weather, on the contrary, can be very clear as industry is distant. The temperature can rise quickly and heatwaves soon cause many of the watercourses to dry up. Given a prolonged heatwave the peat will dry out and crack and even sphagnum moss can become parched. It's a good idea to keep an eye on the changing weather patterns - not just for personal safety, but as an aid to easy progress. Hard frosts and heatwaves make some of the rougher, wetter moorlands easier to negotiate. Hard snow cover is simply a delight as it smooths out all the rough

13

edges. Heavy rain gives added power to already powerful water-falls. On the whole, you'll just have to take the weather as it comes and make, or alter, plans accordingly.

The Helm Wind

THE HELM Wind is the only wind in the country with a proper name and it is restricted to the East Fellside flank of the North Pennines. Many walkers have half-heard of it and make the mistake of thinking that any howling gale must be the Helm Wind. This isn't the case. The Helm Wind is a peculiar wind which relies on a particular set of circumstances for its generation. When all these have been duly noted, the Helm Wind is "on" as they say on the East Fellside.

First of all, there must be a north-easterly wind blowing. This isn't the prevailing wind pattern and it is more likely to occur in Winter and Spring. We can track this air mass as it moves across country from the North Sea. The air needs to be moving in excess of 15mph. The Beaufort Wind Scale describes this as Force 4, or a moderate breeze - nothing spectacular. The air crosses the Tyne gap around Corbridge and gradually gets forced higher and higher. It is pushed above 1,000 feet (300 metres) over Hexhamshire Common. As it crosses the moors around Nenthead the ground level is about 2,000 feet (600 metres). Eventually Cross Fell and its lofty satellites are reached, where the moors almost touch 3,000 feet (900 metres). There are no real gaps in this moorland barrier, which is almost consistently above 2,000 feet (600 metres) for dozens of miles.

As the air has been pushed ever upwards from sea level it will have cooled considerably. Any moisture it was carrying will have condensed to form clouds. The clouds will be most noticeable as they build up above the heights of the East Fellside. This is called the Helm Cap. If the air mass isn't particularly moist the Cap will be white and there isn't likely to be any rain. Very moist air results in a dark cap and plenty of rain.

Let's get back to the air mass, which we left just as it was being pushed over Cross Fell and the rest. The air is not only cooler, but as a result it is also quite dense. As it is pushed over Cross Fell it suddenly runs out of high ground and simply drops like a stone into the Vale of Eden, running full pelt down the East Fellside. This, and only this, is the notorious Helm Wind. With sufficient push behind it and accumulated density it can wreak havoc on the East Fellside. It can wither crops, fell trees and remove anything which isn't tied down. Its noise is peculiar - a sort of low moan or rumble, caused by its varying turbulence. It is noticeable that there are few farms on the East Fellside and all the villages have their backs to the fell.

The air mass then performs some peculiar acrobatics. The static air mass in the Vale of Eden is warmer than the Helm Wind and it stands like a wall against its onslaught. The Helm Wind is forced up and back over on itself. Some mixing of warm and cold air occurs in the aerial vortex and results in the formation of a thin, continuous, twisting bar of cloud which simply hovers in mid-air. This is the Helm Bar - final and conclusive proof that the Helm Wind is "on". The met men have a name for this phenomenon - they call it "rotor streaming".

There is a local saying that no matter how strong the Helm Wind blows, it'll never cross the Eden. The warm and cold air battle it out and much of the energy is expended in aerial acrobatics. Only slight surface breezes are evident by the River Eden - even if trees are being uprooted a few miles away. This is the Helm Wind, tied down by definitions, restricted to its traditional howling grounds until the north-easterly push gives out. It's something to look for while walking on the East Fellside, but don't call it the Helm Wind until all its characteristics have been observed!

Flora

ATTENTION IS usually drawn to the arctic/alpine flora of Upper Teesdale and the profusely flowered haymeadows, but this is rather missing the point. Yes - there are a lot of plants in the area. Yes - there are a lot of rare plants in the area. But - the real question concerns why so many plants from such varied backgrounds should find Upper Teesdale so accommodating. In general terms, the arctic/ alpines are at home there because the climate suits them. The long, hard winters are akin to the better conditions pertaining after the Ice Age. The flower-rich haymeadows thrive because hay-making comes so late in Upper Teesdale and the plants have a chance to drop their seeds beforehand. This is being encouraged to ensure the continuing proliferation of species. Some plants are confined to

15

specific locations because of the character of the soil - particularly the soil generated by the unique "Sugar Limestone". Other plants are actually suited to the toxic spoils unearthed by lead miners and several other plants thrive on disturbed ground.

Many parts of the North Pennines feature vast areas of aptly-named blanket bog. These are deep accumulations of semi-rotted vegetable matter. In some areas there are exposed tree stumps which indicate that there was a vast tree cover in times past. Some of the woodland plants remain, simply adapting to other types of shade. The process of peat formation has undoubtably slowed down and many areas of blanket bog are in a state of decay. Erosion is removing the peat more quickly than it can be built up - hence the appearance of so many areas of peat hags and groughs. Botanical life is at the end of its tether in those areas, but some species find it favourable. In some areas there are springs which seep slowly to the surface and make the peat so sodden that only mosses can take hold. These areas are called flushes and can feature a remarkable concentration of odd species. The mosses, liverworts and lichens are a specialist study and hundreds of colonies of each have been logged.

The heathery moorlands are largely artificial. This type of moorland has been encouraged to form a larger habitat for the ill-fated grouse. The whole of the North Pennines is a managed landscape. Grouse-shooting, sheep grazing and general agriculture have had a dramatic effect on the distribution of flora. It is remarkable that so much of interest has remained - there seems to be a little niche for a bit of everything in this vast landscape, with a host of species adapting to changing conditions and maintaining a roothold in the region despite constant interference.

It has been my intention to write this section without referring to a single species and I see that I have managed it. Writing a list of species which might be noted simply defeats the reason for all the interest in the first place. Use a good field guide or walk with someone who has a good knowledge of the plants and their habitats. Visit the Bowlees Visitor Centre and look at their displays, which include living specimens. After that, search for the elusive spring gentian and delight in the cloudberry cover on the boggy moors and wonder if the mountain pansy is marking the site of an overgrown spoil heap.

Fauna

THERE ARE the Swaledale sheep and Red Grouse. Having disposed of them, there are certain creatures which have a limited habitat - such as a small snail in Upper Teesdale which was once thought to be extinct in this country. Roe deer and squirrels can be spotted with care and patience in some of the surviving woodlands or more recent forests. Feral ponies occur all along the length of the East Fellside flank of the North Pennines. These are no doubt related to the Carrier Galloways used by miners, which are in turn said to be descended from a single pony found wandering in the Vale of Eden after Bonnie Prince Charlie's retreat. Weasels, stoats and foxes can be seen, but are strictly controlled on the grouse moors. Adders and grass snakes have limited habitats and Teesdale is naturally one of them. The large areas of wet moorland feature several areas of stagnant water and it is possible to find frogs, dragonflies and awful midges.

The bird-life is profuse - especially around Geltsdale. The area is on a short coast-to-coast migration route and Geltsdale's varied habitats of open water, moorland and woodland mean that literally anything could drop in. Golden eagles and little bittern have been noted on their travels, which makes listing species rather a pointless exercise. There is no substitute for a first-hand sighting on an actual visit. The RSPB reserve should be high on every ornithologist's list. The usual range of moorland birds include curlew, lapwing, golden plover, snipe, redshank and dunlin. Both the red and black grouse can be seen. Birds of prey are greeted with a mixed response on the grouse moors. Legal protection has been assigned to them, but some species have been persecuted in some areas. The rivers and streams will almost always feature the cheerful dipper and in many areas the heron also feeds. Some species such as crossbills are dependant upon pine nuts and therefore tend to frequent large forestry plantations such as Hamsterley or Slaley. The red grouse isn't the only bird to be given a helping hand - the number of pied flycatchers in Geltsdale was increased through the provision of nesting boxes. Fat pheasants are reared for game and like the red grouse pay the ultimate price! A good field guide is useful to help with identification of unusual species on the walks.

Mining

THE NORTH Pennines was once the world's greatest producer of lead and the subject has been covered exhaustively. Only a brief glance at the industry can be spared here. Firstly, the history of the industry cannot be traced to an origin - the Romans may have started it all, or even their predecessors. The problem is that any early workings would tend to be obscured by later ones in the same areas. The provision of Roman roads through Alston Moor, Teesdale and Weardale suggests that they had an interest in lead mining. Mining was a haphazard occupation in the Middle Ages, but there was some order brought to the industry on Alston Moor, where there was a high proportion of silver in the lead. These were known as the "Silver Mines of Carlisle" and were brought under Crown control. At 40oz of silver per ton of lead there was sufficient reason for the establishment of a Mint at Carlisle to deal with the output.

In general terms, maximum output and development occurred from 1700 to 1900. There were two companies which became pre-eminent in this period. WB Lead Worked Allendale and Weardale and was controlled by the Blackett-Beaumont family. The London Lead Company worked Tynedale, Teesdale and the East Fellside under a directorship whose religion led to the company being known as the "Quaker Company". Not only did the big companies extract and process vast amounts from the mines, but they also improved social conditions and provided facilities for the health and education of their workers. Even so, a miner's life was not always a happy one.

It helps if the general visitor and walker understands something of the lead mining industry. This would allow a greater appreciation of the ruins and remains found on the high moors. A couple of hours spent at any or all of the dalehead Heritage Centres at Allenheads, Killhope Wheel or Nenthead will be most rewarding. The basic processes of lead mining, smelting and transport can be studied. It's helpful to know the difference between a level and a shaft, a buddle and a jigger. Ruined smelt mills and old flues occur on some of the walks and it is useful to know how these refineries worked. Water power was harnessed at practically every site and a knowledge of how watercourses were constructed can be used to determine overgrown specimens across miles of moorlands.

They say it was all the work of "T'Awd Man" - Old Man. When you are walking in mist and stumble upon a ruined mine shop, then that's where T'Awd Man lived. When you discover an overgrown spoil or a half-hidden mine, then that's where T'Awd Man worked. Even when a miner broke into an old, unknown working, he knew that T'Awd Man had beaten him to it. The more you come to understand how T'Awd Man lived and worked on these moors, the more you can feel him looking over your shoulder as you try to piece together the evidence of his life and work.

By all means scramble on the spoil heaps for specimens, and have a look at the old buildings, but remember that all these remains can be very dangerous. Open shafts and levels are subject to sudden collapse and should never be entered except with well-qualified guides. Old buildings can be very tottery and and should be treated with care. Supporting timbers soon rot and give way.

Souvenir specimens of heavy, silvery-grey galena can be picked up from many sites. Hard, bright quartz, broken rhombic pieces of calcite and heavy, white chunks of barytes can be gleaned. There are multi-coloured cubes of fluorspar which catch the eye. Compounds of copper, zinc and iron exist in some places. A field guide will help with the identification of specimens. Alternatively, you could check off your haul against those lodged at the Heritage Centres of museums. Even some pubs have good collections and many families have kept the "bonny bits" gathered by their ancestors. On one of the routes, and I won't say which one, there is a chunk of galena as big as your head embedded in a track. It's a surprise which you might encounter and for a bit of effort it's yours!

Grouse Shooting

THE RED Grouse is a large, well-camouflaged bird which breaks suddenly and alarmingly from underfoot. Its rapid wing beats, long glides and "go-back" call make it instantly recognisable. Around six to 12 well-camouflaged eggs are laid in a heathery scrape in April or May. The chicks feed mainly on insects and are flying in a fortnight. A family group is known as a brood, while larger populations are called packs. Adult birds feed almost exclusively on young heather shoots. Grouse don't migrate, but shelter in deep heather during foul weather and sit out long winters on the moors.

Pest control in Allendale

Vast areas of heather moorlands have been created by selective strip burning. Heather seeds are fairly fire-resistant, but even so the process has to be managed carefully to avoid firing whole moorlands. The burning is controlled from October 1st to April 15th. Strip burning allows young heather shoots to grow, suitable for feeding, alongside deep heather, suitable for shelter. The regeneration of burnt areas can be spoiled by invasive bracken getting the first roothold. Heather cannot tolerate waterlogged ground and in many areas drainage ditches are cut to allow a greater cover to become established.

Crows, foxes, stoats, weasels and latterly mink are all controlled by trapping, shooting and poisoning. Keepers have occasionally been suspected of discouraging predator birds protected by law, but on some estates there is no interference. Once the number of "pests" has been reduced, many other moorland birds find nesting conditions improved and thrive alongside the grouse.

Shooting begins on August 12th - the Glorious Twelfth - and continues as late as December 10th. Some estates take as much as £1,000 a day off sportsmen, while other areas are managed simply for small gun clubs. There is great prestige attached to getting the first grouse on the tables of London restaurants and the whole business seems less of a blood sport and more of a social occasion.

The numbers of people employed on the various estates differs widely. Sometimes there are full-time keepers and others employed in labouring and maintenance. When the shooting season is in full swing there are plenty of part-time jobs such as beating, driving, cooking and bottle-washing to be done. Sections of the local economy are built around the sport of grouse shooting and it is wise for walkers to bear this in mind.

Access

THERE IS a vast amount of open space in the North Pennines and much of it is without rights of way. Some parts may in fact be visited by walkers unless some activity such as shooting is taking place which specifically excludes them. Other parts are managed in a way which simply doesn't tolerate walkers at all. Sorting out the various areas is quite difficult, but it is as well to be aware that there are such differences.

Many of the routes in this guide are entirely along rights of way. A simple check of the appropriate maps will confirm this for prospective walkers. Other routes include tracks or areas of open country which aren't covered by rights of way, but there seems to be no objection to walkers using them. It is common courtesy for walkers, even on rights of way, to allow various countryside processes to be concluded before proceeding. If sheep need to be got through a gate, or shooting is taking place from a series of butts, then wait for a break before continuing. It shouldn't inconvenience you too much to wait a few minutes and a pleasant attitude pays dividends.

Some rights of way seem to be drawn on the map and simply end half-way up a hill or half-way across a moor. It is *generally* safe to assume that the open areas reached are places where the public have a right to "air and exercise" but this may not always be the case.

On some of the more up-market grouse moors there is year-round maintenance. Wherever a series of shooting butts occur on a walk, this fact is mentioned. These may be positioned alongside a right of way, or they may be on routes which aren't covered by a right of way. In either case, it is perhaps best to avoid using such

A forceful statement on access to MOD property at Hilton

routes if local information says that a shoot is taking place. Choose another walk.

The Warcop Training Range is another special case. Access is forbidden while firing is in progress and "clear" days are usually Mondays, which are of little use to many walkers. In the case of the Range, a simple phone call gains information on the state of play.

Vast areas are protected in the name of conservation and access isn't encouraged. Immense National Nature Reserves, Sites of Special Scientific Interest and other areas are barred to walkers. Some officials seem intent on making walkers out to be blundering buffoons, but it is wrong to judge all walkers as if they were oblivious of their surroundings. Most walkers are careful and considerate and if they have the intelligence to complete a wilderness walk they obviously understand something about those areas.

A few of the suggested routes in this guide might be construed as blatant trespass, but that isn't the intention. There are a number of guidebooks, particularly the summit-bagging types, which have covered many of the forbidden heights of the North Pennines. People are already walking in the areas described in this guide. The routes are my statements about routes which I have myself walked. Whether anyone else walks all, some, or none of them is a matter for individual discretion. I would hope that in some of the more sensitive areas, walkers would enjoy themselves in small, quiet groups. Large groups tend to be noisier and more obvious and I would hope that they would stick to the more popular walks and firm trackways, preferably on rights of way. If you are a stickler for the letter of the law, then follow it precisely. Whatever you choose, maintain a respect for the countryside and its inhabitants and a cheerful disposition in the face of conflict.

Public Transport

IT HAS to be said at the outset that travelling by car is by far the most convenient way of getting around the North Pennines. This is a sparsely populated area and public transport is very limited. There is no real problem getting around the perimeter, which is mostly bounded by good rail or bus services, but finding meaningful connections between the dales is difficult. It is pointless to give detailed timetables as operators and times of services are subject to sudden change.

Railways are very peripheral to the North Pennines. The Settle to Carlisle line and the Tyne Valley line can be used to reach places where a bus connection can provide a link with the wilder interior of the North Pennines. The industrial line in Weardale is available to the public as far as Stanhope on summer Sundays only. The South Tynedale Railway is really only a "fun" line.

Alston is a reasonably good centre for buses, with links to the East Fellside, the Allendales, South Tynedale and occasionally Upper Weardale. Buses from Hexham serve the Allendales, Blanchland, Edmundbyers, Consett and Barnard Castle. A number of operators give routes along the lengths of Weardale and Teesdale, becoming less frequent the further into the dales they penetrate. From Barnard Castle there are some services to Bowes, Stainmore and over to the Vale of Eden.

There are a range of small services that are worth knowing about. Many rural parts of Durham are covered by Ruralride buses, which rely on a measure of support from the communities they reach. In the summer there are services to out-of-the way Youth Hostels such as Baldersdale, Langdon Beck and Edmundbyers. Villages such as Holwick and Harwood can be reached. Tours sometimes include visits to Cow Green Reservoir, Hamsterley Forest, Killhope Wheel or even over to Alston. Part of the East Fellside is served by the Fellrunner Community Minibus, which offers routes from the East Fellside villages to and from Carlisle and Penrith. Some guided walks are also offered using the Fellrunner.

If you try hard enough it is possible to find some sort of service to most places - though it might be a limited school run or a seasonal affair. What's really needed is a comprehensive booklet of timetables for the whole of the North Pennines and such a project would surely attract some measure of grant aid, or have its cost of production raised from advertising. Until such a publication appears, the following phone numbers can be used to check the availability of services for each county:

> (0228) 812812 - for routes in Cumbria.
> (0670) 514343 - for routes in Northumberland.
> 091 386 4411   - for routes in Durham.

The Walks

THE WALKS are a mixed bag, but generally speaking they have a bias towards the wide open moorlands and heights. This is what the North Pennines are all about - space, wilderness and exposure to the elements. There are a few easy, low-level walks suitable for the cautious or for use in nasty weather. Many of the higher routes aren't too difficult as they are routed along good clear tracks and paths. Very few of the walks tackle the open moorlands without any navigational aids to follow, such as fences and walls. A few of the walks cover wet or boggy ground. Levels of difficulty are given as easy, moderate or difficult.

Most of the walks are circular, from a given point with a handy parking space, but a few walks are linear and thought needs to be given to transport and pick-ups. The length of the walks varies from four to 13 miles. Ordnance Survey map numbers are quoted which refer to the 1:50,000 Landranger Series, 1:25,000 Pathfinder Series, or the Outdoor Leisure Sheet 31. The sketch maps aren't intended to be a substitute for the Ordnance Survey maps. The sketch maps are drawn fairly simply at a scale of 1:60,000 to enable the routes to be checked on larger scale maps. Always take the suggested maps, which will prove invaluable in cases of difficulty.

An introduction to each walk points out what sort of walk it is, gives basic details about the route, then points out any features of interest which might be worth studying. Some of the walks feature old lead mining remains, or pass through areas with notable wildlife. There might be a transport theme, such as an old road or railway which features prominently. Perhaps the town or village at the start of the walk is worth a closer look.

The route description should be used in conjunction with the appropriate Ordnance Survey maps. These will show, for instance, whether the route is a right of way or not, as well as yielding vital information about the surroundings. The route description is there simply to see the walk through to a successful conclusion, but occasionally refers to a point of interest which might also be covered in the introductory notes. The presence of old mines or shooting butts are given, as these might prove dangerous.

There are 42 day-walks in the guide, then a section of six longer walks presented in outline form only. Those who are new to walking in the North Pennines might like to try and complete one of the day-walks each week throughout a year, using holidays to tackle the longer walks. Anyone completing this plan in a year would certainly know the North Pennines quite well, but would still only be scratching the surface of what the area has to offer in the way of walking opportunities. Walkers who already know the area well may find that I have revealed a corner or two which they haven't yet explored. They might also wonder why their own favourite walk isn't listed - well - neither is mine!

Words Used On Maps

Burns and *becks* are the same thing - minor watercourses which flow into the main rivers. The word *burn* is used for the most part, but on the East Fellside and in most of Teesdale *beck* is used.

Cocklake sounds like there ought to be at least a puddle somewhere on the moor, but *lake* derives from *lek* which is the courtship display of the black grouse. The species traditionally displays on certain parts of the moors and these are indicated as *Cocklakes*. If there are no black grouse in the area, then it's pointless going to a *Cocklake* to see them.

Hopes are pronounced as *ups*. Stanhope, Rookhope, Middlehope and so on become Stanup, Rookup and Middleup. A *hope* is a valley or dale and the term is widely used throughout Weardale and nearby areas.

Knoutberry or *Outberry* on a map refers to the presence of cloudberries on the higher, boggier moors. They may not actually be present if the placename has been in use for a long time, as the plant is becoming less widely distributed and rather scarce in many areas.

Tourist Information Centres

THIS LIST features a number of Tourist Information Centres which are situated on the fringes of the North Pennines, as there are only a few within the region.

Tourist Information Centre, Railway Station, Alston. (0434) 381696
Tourist Information Centre, Moot Hall, Appleby. (07683) 51177
Tourist Information Centre, Galgate, Barnard Castle. (0833) 690909
Tourist Information Centre, Moot Hall, Brampton. (06977) 3433
Tourist Information Centre, One Stop Shop, Brough. (09304) 260
Tourist Information Centre, Hallgates, Hexham. (0434) 605225
Tourist Information Centre, Market Square, Kirkby Stephen.
    (07683) 71199
Tourist Information Centre, Craft Shop, Middleton. (0833) 40400
Tourist Information Centre, Church Bank, Shotley Bridge.
    (0207) 591043
Tourist Information Centre, Dales Centre, Stanhope. (0388) 527650

Other useful contacts include the following:

Bowes Museum, Barnard Castle. (0833) 690606
Weardale Museum of High House Chapel, Ireshopeburn.
    (0388) 537417
Killhope Wheel Lead Mining Centre, Killhope.
    (0388) 537505 (Winter 091-386-4411 ex 2354)
Hamsterley Forest Information Centre. (0388) 88312
Bowlees Visitor Centre. (0833) 2292
Allenheads Heritage Centre. (0434) 685395
Warcop Training Range, Warcop. (09304) 661
Talkin Tarn Country Park, Brampton. (06977) 3129
RSPB, Geltsdale Reserve. (0228) 70205

Geltsdale Section

WALK 1:   Brampton, Gelt and Talkin
WALK 2:   Croglin and Croglin Fell
WALK 3:   Midgeholme and Cold Fell

I'm giving Geltsdale a clear identity in this guide. It's worth noting its Sunday name - the King's Forest of Geltsdale - a pointer to royal patronage. The area is at the north-western end of the North Pennines, not far from main road and rail services, but remaining aloof and remote. The three walks chosen to represent Geltsdale could in truth be placed in other sections. Croglin Fell is really part of the East Fellside; Cold Fell extends sprawling shoulders into South Tynedale; and Brampton is rather peripheral to the North Pennines in any case. Together, they allow a peep into Geltsdale - the dale of the "mad" river, vampire attacks and an ornithologist's paradise.

WALK 1: BRAMPTON, GELT AND TALKIN

Brampton is a reasonable gateway to the North Pennines, giving access to Geltsdale, South Tynedale and the East Fellside. The immediate countryside is gentle, though full of surprises. This walk leads from Brampton, wanders up Geltsdale, then has a look at Talkin Tarn before returning to Brampton. It's an easy, low-level walk on good paths and roads with no difficulties.

There is a Roman fort site close to the River Irthing and Brampton originally grew there. The area was cleared and the village was transferred to its present site, where it grew as a market town. A Moot Hall has stood in the centre of town since 1648, but the present octagonal building, which houses the Tourist Information Centre, dates from 1817. This was a fiercely contested Border area for centuries, ending with the arrival of Bonnie Prince Charlie on his white charger. Brampton was his headquarters in 1745 during the

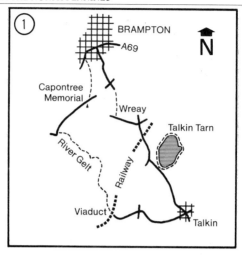

siege of Carlisle. The mayor and aldermen of Carlisle eventually journied to Brampton to hand over the keys of the city. A proud, but short-lived moment for the Prince. After his retreat six notable supporters were strung from the branches of the Capon Tree outside town. The tree takes its name from the capons eaten by the assize judges travelling to Carlisle. They were in the habit of breaking their journey at the tree in order to accept bribes from litigants in advance of court proceedings. Have a good look around Brampton, searching out St. Martin's Church, Prince Charlie's House, the old stocks, the site of an old bullring and sundry fine buildings. The Capon Tree has gone; replaced by a stone memorial in 1904.

The River Gelt is fascinating and its name is supposedly derived from "geilt" - meaning mad. They call it the Mad River and it certainly looks the part. Moments of sudden fury and frenzy occur where the river has cut a tortuous channel out of the soft red sandstone. This easily worked stone has not gone unnoticed. Romans quarried it to repair Hadrian's Wall and left their mark on a rock face known as the "Written Rock of Gelt". Expert guidance is needed to locate and translate the script. Abraham's Cave, cut in 1814, became a lair for miscreants. Hell Beck, a tributary of the Gelt, ran red for three days after a battle in 1570. One of the earliest skewed viaducts in the country spans Geltsdale and was completed in 1853. The masonry is reputed to have been planned by using carved turnips to model the shapes of the stones. The varied woodlands of Geltsdale are managed by the RSPB and provide a home to a populous birdlife, including wood warblers, treecreepers, pied flycatchers, woodpeckers, songthrushes, blackcaps and so on. Roe deer and red squirrels can be spotted with patience. Mosses, liverworts, fungi and ferns thrive in damp, shady spots. Linger long in Geltsdale.

Talkin Tarn Country Park is seldom quiet. A number of watersports are permitted, but swimming is discouraged as the water rises from subterranean sources and is rather cold. There are legends here which have counterparts elsewhere. An angel of God, ill-treated by an entire village, save for one old widow, caused the tarn to drown all but the old dear (*cf.* Semerwater in the Dales). Some say the tarn is bottomless, while others contradict this and say that on stormy nights the church bells of the drowned village toll beneath the waves. There's more - the tarn has the power of speech, as in Talking Tarn! The walking is pleasant and the view is pretty, but if you want to spot birds you're at the wrong tarn. Try nearby Tindale Tarn, where it's much quieter, with less hype and more wildlife.

THE ROUTE

Distance:	An easy nine mile low-level walk on good paths and roads.
Maps:	1:50,000 Landranger Sheet 86
	1:25,000 Pathfinder Sheets 545 & 558
Start/Finish:	Brampton
Getting There:	Brampton is on the A69 between Carlisle and Hexham. It can also be reached via the A689 from Alston.
Parking:	In Brampton.

Leave Brampton by following Elmfield, which is the name of the busy A69 leaving town for Carlisle. A short way along the road, on the left, is a footpath sign for the Capontree Memorial. Follow this path through fields for ¹/₂ mile to reach a minor road. A right turn quickly leads to the memorial, which is on the left by a minor junction. The road continues another $^1/_2$ mile to Low Geltbridge. The Bonnie Prince travelled this way to reach Carlisle as it was the main highway at that time. Don't cross the bridge, but turn left to follow the River Gelt upstream through woodlands.

The paths alongside the Gelt are well maintained, but a network of other trails allow the woodlands to be explored in some detail if required. Remain close to the river for $1^3/_4$ miles. Take the opportunity to study the rock channels and potholed river bed, but beware of slippery rocks near the river's edge. A small bridge crosses the infamous Hell Beck and the path continues upstream to reach a minor road. The Middle Gelt Viaduct spans Geltsdale at this point. The names of the builder and engineer are inscribed in Latin and English on opposite piers. Don't cross the bridge over the river, but walk uphill by road for $1^1/_4$ miles, passing straight through a crossroads to reach Talkin village. There are a couple of pubs in this neat and attractive village, but if neither is required, simply turn left and follow the road for $^3/_4$ mile to reach the Tarn End Hotel.

A short path alongside the Hotel gives access to the shore of Talkin Tarn. There is a footpath which makes a complete circuit and all the walker needs to do is decide which way round to walk - clockwise or anti-clockwise. If this decision requires a lot of thought, then relax on the tarn-side lawn of the Hotel with a drink and consider the options. Fields and woodlands fringe the tarn and while the scene is pretty, sheer numbers of visitors seem to keep the wildlife at bay. When explorations are over, rejoin the road near the Hotel to continue.

Turn right and walk along the road, then right again to follow the B6413 for $^1/_2$ mile. Turn left at a minor crossroads to reach Wreay. Turn right here to pick up a path across fields to gain the top end of Brampton. Walk straight downhill by road to return to the centre of town.

An alternative start and finish are available for anyone arriving by train at Brampton Station. Start by walking down into town, then continue the route as described. On reaching Talkin Tarn, the walk can be ended as follows: Walk into the woods behind the boathouses and head for the fence at the edge of the woods. A small gate leads into a field and Brampton Station is in view from there. Walk across fields to reach a minor road, then turn right to follow the road to the station.

WALK 2: CROGLIN AND CROGLIN FELL

Croglin is a little-known, but attractive red sandstone village at the foot of a series of wild moorlands. This walk wanders through the village, then takes a track practically to the summit of Croglin Fell. The ascent is therefore easy, but the continuation is over rough moorlands and involves fording a river twice. After leaving the hills the walking becomes easier, using a low-level route to link Newbiggin and Croglin. After heavy rain the fords would still be passable, but would certainly result in wet feet. In such conditions it might be a good idea to choose a different walk.

When a moorland is managed for grouse-shooting it is sometimes the case that access tracks are constructed much faster than the map-makers can hope to record them. Croglin Fell has more miles of such routes than the map admits. Walkers using these new routes can walk with ease over moorlands which were formerly quite difficult to negotiate. There are no forbidding notices along this route, but note that rights of way exist only on the lower slopes of the fell. One

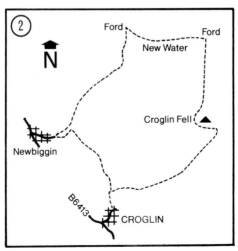

of the access tracks is used to gain the summit of Croglin Fell and another one is used in the valley of New Water, close to where an outcrop of the Whin Sill causes a set of waterfalls.

Croglin is a very quiet village, yet some twenty years before Bram Stoker unleashed *Dracula* on an unsuspecting world, this place was experiencing a series of vampire attacks. Bram Stoker was only writing a story, of course, but the exploits of the "Croglin Bat" were reported in no less an organ than the *Gentleman's Magazine* as chilling fact. It all started in 1875 when an Australian family took the tenancy of Croglin Low Hall. Amelia Cranswell was the name of the hapless maiden - attacked in her bedroom by a demonic figure reeking of decay and clad only in a black grave-shroud. It burst through her window and left immediately after biting her face and neck. A doctor pronounced her injuries to be the work of some beast - not a human.

The Cranswells packed and left for a holiday in Switzerland. One can only wonder at what possessed them to return to Croglin Low Hall, but this time a number of precautions were taken. The Bat appeared to be at work elsewhere, judging from odd rumours which drifted around the countryside, but when it did eventually return to Croglin Low Hall it was pursued and shot. It managed to escape by descending into an old crypt. Several well armed villagers opened the crypt in the morning and discovered a ghastly decomposed body with blood-stained fangs. Using a stake of that mystical tree - the rowan - the Bat's heart was pierced and for good measure the coffin and its grisly contents were put to the torch.

Whoever, or whatever the Croglin Bat was, or wherever the crypt was, neither seems to have any connection with Croglin's pleasant little church. The more you delve into this story, or any like it, the more inconsistencies and dead ends are found. What of the bricked up window at Croglin Hall - once Amelia's bedroom window? Another case of avoiding window tax, perhaps? Whatever the truth behind it all, it's a good tale in keeping with the character of the area, but one you might have preferred not to know with darkness falling in the wilds beyond Croglin Fell.

Hard frosts make some of the moorlands easier to negotiate

Wild flowers and thistledown

Killhope Wheel Lead Mining Centre
Bernard's castle and the County Bridge

THE ROUTE

Distance:	A moderate ten mile moorland walk involving river fords.
Maps:	1:50,000 Landranger Sheet 86
	1:25,000 Pathfinder Sheets 558 & 568
Start/Finish:	Croglin
Getting There:	Croglin can be reached via the B6413 from Brampton or the B6412 from Langwathby.
Parking:	Small spaces in the village.
	Ask permission if in doubt.

Start by following the road opposite the Robin Hood pub to walk through the village of Croglin. After admiring the pleasant red sandstone cottages and the church, continue past an old quarry and turn left to walk steeply uphill for ¼ mile. Take the next turning on the right to follow an obvious gravel track across the flank of Croglin Fell. After climbing for two miles the track reaches a gate and divides to serve the grouse moors. Turn left to walk towards the summit of Croglin Fell. The track deteriorates without actually reaching the topmost point. A short climb takes in the 1,940 feet (591 metres) trig point and allows the heathery humps of Geltsdale to be studied. Far away across the Vale of Eden are the shapelier fells of the Lake District and in clear weather Criffell can be seen across in Scotland.

Aim roughly northwards to descend. An old ditch and a sparse line of fenceposts lead downhill. This line continues more steeply downhill alongside an old wall which has been converted into a series of shooting butts. A sudden further steepening of the slope finally leads down to New Water, about a mile from the summit of Croglin Fell. There is no bridge over the river, so a practicable ford must be found. In conditions of normal flow it is just possible for booted walkers to get across dry-shod. Wet weather will almost certainly mean wet feet.

A track which isn't marked on the map runs roughly parallel to New Water. Climb up to the track, turn left and follow it gently downhill. There are a couple of waterfalls in the river which warrant a slight detour. After a mile the track moves well away from the river and swings to the right. This is the time to branch off to the left and walk through a brackeny area to get back down to the river. Maps show a bridleway crossing New Water and walkers who can locate that point will discover that it was once bridged. Alas, only a single stone abutment remains, which means fording the river again. (It is perhaps necessary to point out that it is easier done this way than trying to avoid crossing the river at all.)

Climbing southwards from New Water, follow a wet and boggy track. This becomes better with distance and was obviously quite a good thoroughfare in its day. Two shooting huts will be noticed on the right, well above the track. An improved surface has been laid down to allow vehicular access from Newbiggin, which is the route taken to descend from the hills. Notice a large limekiln on the left before the track runs downhill in earnest. It is a mile down to Newbiggin and the village has a pub if anyone wants a break before returning to Croglin. If not, then don't enter the village, but turn left for Town Head Farm Stables. Don't go into the farmyard, but follow a track uphill parallel to the one just used for the descent. Turn right after ¼ mile and follow a good track across the lower slopes of Croglin Fell for over a mile. This joins a track used on the outward journey. Simply turn right, then left to go down to Croglin and walk back through the village to the Robin Hood pub.

WALK 3: MIDGEHOLME AND COLD FELL

Cold Fell is the most northerly of the North Pennines - a final, proud, whaleback rise before the lowland pastures of the Tyne Gap. Its nipple-like summit tumulus makes it a landmark for miles around, though an elderly Geltsdale farmer asked me to point it out as he'd heard the name but wasn't sure where it was! Its name speaks of winter and its position must surely lay it open to chilly breezes. The burghers of Carlisle certainly look on its snowy form long after the plains have thawed. Cold by name - cold by nature.

It comes as no surprise to learn that a difficult walk is in store. The easiest ascent is from Forest Head, but the one given here is a tougher circuit from Midgeholme and Halton Lea Gate. Both villages are outposts of their respective counties of Cumbria and Northumberland. Halton has a shop, but that's about all in the way of tourist concessions. There are no rights of way over any part of the

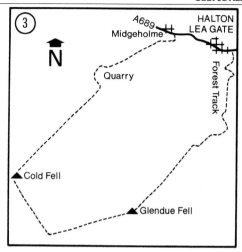

route described below. For the most part the route is across wild and unfrequented moorlands, but a couple of access tracks have been pressed into service to allow a fairly easy entry and exit. A forest track is used to gain height from Halton and cut out rough, bracken-clad fellsides. An old quarry track is used to return to Midgeholme. There are fences crossing the whole of Cold Fell and its satellites. These are obstacles at first, but then become faultless guides in poor visibility. If rain and mist should blot out the view while the walk is in progress, then so be it. If those conditions pertain at the outset, then choose a walk somewhere else. Cold Fell can be a treadmill in bad weather, but it provides an interesting and testing walk in good weather.

The Pennine Way touches only the fringes of Cold Fell and its outliers. It lies far to the east, skulking along the foot of Glendue Fell and Hartleyburn Common following the remains of the Maiden Way Roman road. Wayfarers don't particularly enjoy that section, but maybe only one in a thousand wonders whether Cold Fell offers anything better. Very, very rarely someone branches off the Pennine Way to find out, rejoining the route wiser for the experience. Good luck to them. Most other walkers are summit baggers, mopping up the last of their 2,000 feet summits.

Parts of these vast moorlands are an SSSI and parts are managed by the RSPB, along with Tindale Tarn and the Gelt woodlands. Altogether, these offer a varied selection of habitats on a coast-to-coast migration route. Literally any bird could be passing and no two days will feature the same populations. The usual moorland birds include grouse, curlew, golden plover, dunlin, lapwing and so on. There was an instance when someone, presumably fearing for grouse stocks, deliberately stamped out the nests of hen harriers, including eggs and chicks: the act was accomplished despite vigilance.

An interesting range of plants may be noticed, including a few which people think are restricted to Teesdale. More noticeable are four species which seem to be vying for dominance on the wetter parts of the moor. Heather, bilberry, cloudberry and bog cotton add colour and polka dots to the boggy saddle between Great Blacklaw Hill and Cold Fell. The autumn crop of berries can be particularly rich and a diligent search might reveal oddities such as cranberries.

THE ROUTE

Distance:	A difficult 11 mile moorland walk largely without paths.
Maps:	1:50,000 Landranger Sheet 86
	1:25,000 Pathfinder Sheet 559
Start/Finish:	Midgeholme
Getting There:	Midgeholme is on the A689 between Brampton and Alston.
	It can also be reached by minor roads from Haltwhistle.
Parking:	A small space opposite the phone box at Midgeholme.

Midgeholme is in Cumbria and from the parking space near the phone box the county boundary sign for Northumberland can be seen. Walk across the boundary and continue for a mile along the A689. This is known as Pennine Road at Halton Lea Gate. On leaving this sturdy, stone village, a gate on the right gives access to a forest. Simply walk easily uphill for about two miles on an obvious forest track. At the very end of the track, turn right and walk along a short fire-break to reach the boundary fence and wild moorlands.

As a springboard to higher ground, the forest track is useful and cuts out the rugged lower fellsides. There are no easy routes to Cold Fell. The actual summit is over $2^{1}/_{2}$ miles west of the forest, but a direct line is impractical. A route of $3^{1}/_{2}$ miles can be constructed as follows: Walk south-west to use Glendue Fell as a "stepping-stone". There are no paths on this moorland and fences should be crossed, rather than followed. Continue westwards to the shallow gap between Great Blacklaw Hill and Cold Fell. The boggy moorland features heather, bilberry, cloudberry and bog cotton.

On reaching the shallow gap, turn right and walk north-westwards for a mile. A new fence accompanied by the line of an older fence leads directly to the 2,014 feet (621 metres) summit of Cold Fell. A large tumulus cairn, no doubt the resting place of some chieftain of note, lies sprawled across the summit. A tremendous vista looks out over the Tyne Gap and the Vale of Eden, taking in distant hill groups beyond the pastoral patchwork. In very clear weather some of the highest hills of the Southern Uplands of Scotland can be discerned, while the Cheviots rise above the bristly rug of the Border Forest. Closer to hand is the crest of the Whin Sill which carries Hadrian's Wall from coast-to-coast. The fells of the Lake District are often prominent, while the moorlands of the North Pennines roll backwards in huge, heathery swells.

Three fences meet at the summit of Cold Fell - all useful guides in mist. Take the fence running north-eastwards as a line of descent. In $1^{3}/_{4}$ miles this leads faultlessly down to Black Burn, showing the way across ground which could prove awkward in mist. Treat Black Burn with caution as it is quickly swallowed into a deep, rocky gorge. There is a waterfall worth seeing by those with time and energy to spare. To by-pass this obstacle, don't cross the burn until it has been followed downstream to a safe ford below the gorge. Climb uphill to a prominent spoil heap, which marks the position of an old quarry. Follow the wide access track away from the quarry. This leads gently downhill to Midgeholme in $1^{1}/_{4}$ miles. The final part of the descent runs alongside an old railway and down a farm track, reaching the A689 quite close to the phone box at Midgeholme.

South Tynedale Section

South Tynedale is a slough of despond for many Pennine Wayfarers, who are confined to fiddly field paths with only the odd view of the higher moors. Alston is the major centre, with all services and facilities. It's a remarkable town set on a steep, cobbled street. Slaggyford and Garrigill, like Alston, lie on the Pennine Way, but offer only limited services to travellers. One of the walks explores the moors above Slaggyford; another keeps fairly low between Alston and Garrigill; while the third technically starts on the East Fellside and explores the upper reaches of the Tees and Tyne. One way or another, each walk includes a stretch of the River South Tyne and offers different perspectives on its dale.

WALK 4: SLAGGYFORD AND TOM SMITH'S STONE

Tom Smith's Stone is a name on the map and a stone in a God-forsaken wilderness. It makes something to head for on a long moorland walk, given a good clear day for the expedition. In fact, there are plenty of guides crossing the moors and these are particularly useful in poor visibility, though in rain and mist the walk would be a laborious treadmill. A good track leaves Slaggyford to take walkers to the moors, then a fence acts as a guide towards Tom Smith's Stone. A couple of prominent burns lead off the moor and the Pennine Way provides a link to complete the circuit by returning to Slaggyford. It sounds simple, but it is a long way and some of the ground consists of heather moors and tussocky grass which can be quite tiring. Summit baggers have the option of making an ascent of Grey Nag, enabling them to tick off yet another peak.

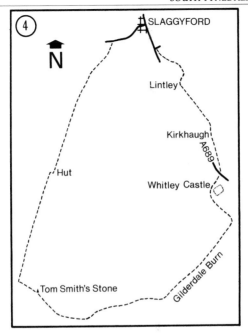

There seem to be no clues as to the identity of Tom Smith. Maybe he was the man who decreed that a stone would be planted in such a desolate spot, or maybe he was the poor navvy charged with getting the thing up there and planted the right way round. It must *have* a right way round as its four sides are carved with the letters A C K & W which are not only neatly alphabetical, but would seem to correspond to the territories of Alston, Croglin, Knarsdale and Whitley. Obviously someone once thought that it was necessary to raise a stone where no-one would see it, and now that it is an established part of the moors it might as well be the object of some attention, though there are no rights of way to it.

Slaggyford was on the branch line which served Alston and it still has its old station house. This actually looks the part as there is a rusty old engine parked alongside! The South Tynedale Railway at Alston has been constructed along the old trackbed, but stops

A waterfall in Gilderdale Burn

well short of Slaggyford. Perhaps one day the railway will be fully open as a "fun" line. In the meantime, Slaggyford slumbers. There is a little circular railway which has been constructed around the caravan site beside the river - a jolly little thing which runs through ornamental grounds.

The Roman fort of Whitley Castle is mildly interesting. Its situation is more inspiring than the actual remains, which consist of a series of concentric grassy ramparts around a central platform. It is outstanding in that it was the only major fort to be constructed within the North Pennines - there are plenty of quite famous forts situated around the fringes. It could be that the Romans were involved in mining the lead of Alston Moor, but that is difficult to prove as later workings would tend to obscure earlier ones. It's unlikely that the Maiden Way would have been constructed through Alston Moor and South Tynedale without a very good reason behind it. Another Roman high-road links Teesdale and Weardale - another area of substantial lead deposits. During excavations at Whitley Castle, a large midden was unearthed, which the farmer of that time promptly put to use for manuring his fields! It isn't possible to say exactly how close the Pennine Way and Maiden Way are aligned in this part of South Tynedale, but they pursue similar courses from Whitley Castle to Slaggyford. It's become noticeable that many Pennine Wayfarers have started abandoning the trail and make use of the old railway trackbed in these parts.

THE ROUTE

Distance:	A difficult 12 mile moorland walk with an easy finish
Maps:	1:50,000 Landranger Sheet 86
	1:25,000 Pathfinder Sheets 559 & 569
Start/Finish:	Slaggyford
Getting There:	Slaggyford is on the A689 between Alston and Brampton
Parking:	Spaces around the village green

Walk uphill from Slaggyford's spacious green to reach the old railway station. This is easily identified as it has an old engine parked alongside. Cross the trackbed at this point and walk uphill along a minor road for ¹/₂ mile. As soon as the road starts to descend, turn left to follow a gravel track uphill, then take the next track on the right. This track is enclosed between walls and leads in a straight line for two miles to reach a hut at its very end. A gate beside the hut gives access to open moorlands.

Go through the gate, then look out for a nearby fence which continues pointing in roughly the same direction as the track. This provides a faultless guide in poor visibility and is a useful feature to follow even in fine weather. There are two structures to look out for on the moor during the walk. One is the old shepherd's bothy of High Shield, which lies a short way downhill from the fence. The other is a chimney stack belonging to a demolished shooting hut, which lies a short way uphill from the fence. A wall replaces the line of the fence, but keeps running in the same direction to reach a confluence of small burns. A ruined fence leads uphill on a heathery slope. There are enough fenceposts remaining to make this a clear guide as height is gained. Continue in a straight line to come against a well-maintained fence which is aligned to the Northumberland and Cumbria county boundary. Turn left to walk a short way to a junction of three fences. Tom Smith's Stone, all forlorn, stands there about two miles from the hut at the end of the track. There are small patches of cloudberry in the heather.

This junction of fences is useful for anyone wanting to know about safe routes through this wilderness. The one running north-eastwards shows the way to the summit of Grey Nag, for those inclined to make an ascent. The fence running roughly north-westwards ultimately reaches Cold Fell after many miles of difficult moorland has been covered. The other fence leads roughly southwards to Black Fell and the Hartside Road. These are all options to bear in mind for longer expeditions, but for the moment Tom Smith's Stone, at 2.071 feet (631 metres), will serve as an objective in its own right. If the stone indeed marks the boundaries of four areas, why are there only three fences? Walk south-westwards and a line of rotting fenceposts will be revealed - the fourth boundary fence and the key to the descent.

Follow the old fence-line at first, but avoid being drawn too close to Woldgill Burn and later Gilderdale Burn. The easiest walking remains on the Northumberland side throughout. Walk downstream for 3$^1/_2$ miles across pathless ground to reach a blue painted footbridge over Gilderdale Burn. Don't cross the bridge, which brings the Pennine Way across, but turn left to walk uphill to Whitley Castle. Walk past the grassy ramparts of the old fort, then descend to the farmyard at Castle Nook. Turn left on the A689, then immediately right after a phone box. The route through fields is sparsely signposted, with enough hints and clues to keep Pennine Wayfarers on course past Dyke House, Kirkhaugh and Lintley. The route goes under the old railway viaduct at Lintley and follows the River South Tyne back towards Slaggyford, entering the village by road. The Pennine Way, as followed from Gilderdale Burn to Slaggyford, measures four miles.

WALK 5: ALSTON AND GARRIGILL

Alston is a fascinating town set high above the River South Tyne and proudly proclaiming itself to be the highest market town in England. The walk starts at the bottom end of town and finishes at the top. In between times it wanders upstream on the River South Tyne, tracing the Pennine Way to Garrigill. The return is accomplished on a parallel route, seldom more than $^1/_4$ mile from the Pennine Way, but packed with features unknown to Wayfarers; including a peep at the wooded innards of Nattrass Gill and the hoary old farmstead of Annatt Walls, where the inhabitants were once "careful to arrange axes and other weapons at the heads of their beds in order to be in readiness to defend their property against the Scots."

Many Pennine Wayfarers, will have had a hard time on Cross Fell and have no thought other than to reach Alston's Youth Hostel. It's a good enough base from which to explore the town, working gradually uphill on a cobbled street which makes a simple shopping trip seem like a major expedition. There are several interesting shops and access to St. Augustine's Church. The Market Cross - a sort of roof on pillars affair - was a gift in 1765 of William Stephenson - an Alston man who became Mayor of London. It has been demolished by runaway lorries on the steep road, not once, but twice, so take care! Several buildings erected by public subscription shows that the people of Alston have always been willing to chip in towards the common good. Wandering around the back alleys is

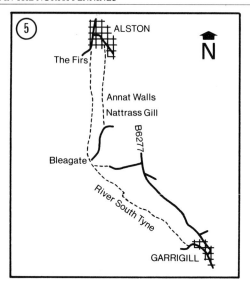

quite interesting, as there are many quaint corners to explore. The Butts is an area which has been re-developed, and was formerly an area for archery practice. It leads onto Gossipgate for a pleasant stroll. Pathways and steps lead back down to the lower part of Alston, where the old railway station is sited - housing the Tourist Information Centre. A short length of the old trackbed has been revitalised as the South Tynedale Railway - a miniature railway which is planned to extend further down-dale in time. The Youth Hostel is quite modern, situated at the start of the walk.

Garrigill is an interesting village worth an hour's exploration, or longer if you get drawn into the pub. The village green is quite spacious and planted with mature trees. St. John's Church has been restored, like so many other churches with an ancient history, but it has managed to retain items from its past. Garrigill was once practically without accommodation for Pennine Wayfarers, which caused the Vicar to throw open the doors of the church in order to provide at least a roof over the heads of hapless wanderers. Now the situation is much improved.

Nattrass Gill is a little fold in the hill which holds charms which cannot be appreciated except at close quarters. There are small waterfalls, wild flowers and tree cover for shade-loving plants such as wood sorrel, ramsons and dainty ferns. One can but feel sorrow for the weary Wayfarers who might even be within earshot, but know nothing of Nattrass Gill.

THE ROUTE

Distance:	An easy nine mile low-level walk on good paths and roads.
Maps:	1:50,000 Landranger Sheets 86 or 87 1:25,000 Outdoor Leisure Sheet 31
Start/Finish:	Alston
Getting There:	Alston is reached from Penrith or Hexham (A686), Brampton or Weardale (A689) or Teesdale (B6277).
Parking:	At the old railway station.

Follow signs for Alston Youth Hostel, situated at the bottom end of town close to the River South Tyne near the main road bridge. Just below the Hostel is a wooded pathway. A plaque reads: "The Firs. This woodland walk belongs to the people of Alston Moor." The way forward is perfectly obvious and the variety of trees in this narrow strip is surprising. At the end of the wood the Pennine Way continues through a series of fields. It is not always particularly well trodden, but the heavily reinforced stiles serve to mark it, as do painted arrows. Nattrass Gill is crossed, but is hardly noticed. Signposts show the way through the farmyard at Bleagate, then the Pennine Way gradually moves closer to the River South Tyne and finally crosses it by a footbridge. Continuing upstream, notice the level bedrock in the river. Look out for dippers along this stretch. After passing a small spoil heap the path leads onto a road. Turn left to follow the road into Garrigill, 4½ miles from Alston.

After exploring Garrigill's wide green, chapels, church and pub, cross the River South Tyne by road to leave. Turn left once across the bridge and walk by road past the new cemetery. Although a riverside path can be picked up at this point, continue uphill by road for another mile to reach the B6277. This gives a panoramic view of South Tynedale which cannot be appreciated from the riverside.

Tynehead Fell, Cross Fell, Melmerby Fell and Black Fell are all featured along the dale.

Turn left off the B6277 and walk downhill past High Plains Lodge Outdoor Education Centre. Continue past Sillyhall, then just as the tarmac ends near Meadow Flatt, turn left through a gate. A vague path leads down almost to Bleagate (passed earlier in the walk), but with luck walkers could find themselves drawn along an old hollow way which is filled with the sort of junk which would send an antique dealer into ecstasies. Whichever course is followed, the Pennine Way will be encountered and should be followed to Bleagate by turning right.

This time, leave Bleagate via its access road by turning right. Follow the road uphill for ¹/₂ mile past Woodstock to reach the access road for High Nest. Turn left through the gateway at this point, then immediately right to climb a stile. A set of stiles marked with fading coloured tape show the way forward to Nattrass Gill, its waterfalls, woodlands, wildlife and beauty. Steps lead in and out of the gill, with a footbridge to keep feet dry. Climbing from the gill, a wide gravel lane is joined at the nearby farmstead of Annatt Walls. Spend a while admiring the sturdy buildings of this one-time hamlet, then walk along the lane. The way to Alston is straight ahead, but there are diversions and distractions in the form of quarry and mining remains, or farm buildings of character. A tarmac footpath finally cuts a corner off a tarmac road and leads more directly to Front Street. The walk down the cobbles allows the shops to be viewed, or a handy pub or hotel to be selected for a drink and a rest. If shopping, be sure to plan your purchase in advance, lest you discover that what you really need is somewhere back at the top of town!

WALK 6: THE KNOCKERGILL PASS

There is a trans-Pennine bridleway known as the Knockergill Pass, whose name seems to be a corruption of Knock Ore Gill which runs between Knock Fell and Great Dun Fell. The route links the East Fellside village of Knock with the Tynedale village of Garrigill, which is a total distance of 13 miles. The journey can be shortened, and much of the road-walking omitted, by having the assistance of

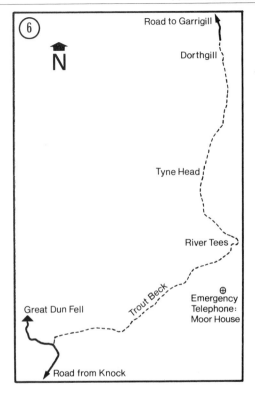

a non-walking motorist friend. The distance can be cut to eight miles if you can persuade someone to drive you up the Great Dun Fell road and meet you on the other side of the Pennines on the Tynehead Fell road.

The walk uses good tracks and paths to explore Trout Beck, which is a feeder of the River Tees, and the River South Tyne. In the distant past Scottish cattle were driven over the pass, while miners used the same route to travel to and from the "shops" or mine lodgings. The pass has found other uses in modern times. The Tynehead Fell road was patched up to enable Moor House to be reached more easily by scientific teams and others engaged in

47

protracted studies in the area. The line from Knock has been replaced by a road which has been built to the very summit of Great Dun Fell - 2,780 feet (847 metres). This was for the construction and maintenance of a series of masts, now replaced by a giant 'radome' which serves to identify the fell in distant views. The rest of the track is little used and in places Trout Beck has swallowed chunks of it.

The Great Dun Fell road is private. Motorists drawn to make an ascent of Britain's highest road find a barrage of notices, including one which points out where your motoring insurance becomes invalid. However, there appears to be a grudging permission for vehicles to be driven to 2,200 feet (670 metres) which is the junction of the Great Dun Fell road with the Silverband Mine road. Having got a walker to this point, the motorist would then be faced with a 30 mile drive to a rendezvous on the Tynehead Fell road.

In the meantime, the walker can appreciate the sheer scale and wilderness quality of the Moor House National Nature Reserve. This is also designated as a World Biosphere Reserve, which means that many studies undertaken there are processed alongside those obtained at other worldwide reserves. Checks can be made on subtle changes in climate and distribution of flora and fauna. Teams of botanists have braved all weathers to check the area with a fine-tooth comb. Nearly 300 flowering plants, over 250 mosses and 100 lichens have been recorded in what appears to be a vast area of grass and heather. This immense blanket bog has little niches where a host of specialised plants can thrive, but some of those which might be noticed include mountain pansy, grass of Parnassus, starry saxifrage, bird's eye primrose, thyme, tormentil and eyebright. Although Moor House once served as a shooting lodge, grouse are no longer game. Other birds include lapwing, curlew, snipe, dunlin, golden plover and ring ouzel. Dippers can be seen in the rivers.

The Tynehead area was mined extensively and for a long time. This was where the "Silver Mines of Carlisle" were located and a persistent rumour relates that a little gold was also won. Lead was the main prize, though copper, zinc and iron have also been extracted. This varied selection results from a mineral-filled fault-line up to 300 feet (90 metres) wide in places. Geological maps call this the Great Sulphur Vein, but the miners called it the "Backbone of the Earth". All that remain are pock-marked moors, overgrown spoil heaps and ruined buildings. Some of the miners were farmers and vice versa. They built a lime kiln by the Tynehead Fell road and improved the moorland, but the moor is now reclaiming its own.

THE ROUTE

Distance:	An easy eight mile moorland walk on good paths and tracks.
Maps:	1:50,000 Landranger Sheet 91
	1:25,000 Outdoor Leisure Sheet 31
Start:	On the Great Dun Fell road
Finish:	On the Tynehead Fell road
Getting There:	The Great Dun Fell road is reached from Knock. The Tynehead Fell road is reached from Garrigill.
Parking:	Very limited on the Great Dun Fell road. Plenty of space beside the Tynehead Fell road.

With the aid of a non-walking motorist friend, start high on the Great Dun Fell road at the junction with the Silverband Mine road. Follow the tarmac road uphill for ½ mile to a battered barrier gate at 2,500 feet (760 metres). Turn right to follow a stony track across the flank of Great Dun Fell. Views into Upper Teesdale are very good. The track runs downhill through an area of spoil heaps, then follows the course of Trout Beck closely. Parts of the old track have been washed away, so try and keep to the left bank to avoid having to cross the river when it has gathered more force. Small notices planted by the Nature Conservancy ask walkers to keep to the path. Trout Beck becomes ever more powerful and attractive and displays a fine set of falls close to a bridge, over three miles down from the Great Dun Fell road.

The bridge gives access to Moor House - the centre of the Moor House Reserve. Visitors are not encouraged, but in case of emergency attention is drawn to a telephone in the yard of the house, but this facility must not be abused.

Follow the access road away from Moor House and cross the nearby River Tees. This is already a substantial river, though it hasn't flowed much further than Trout Beck. The surface of the access road varies from tarmac to gravel and is perfectly obvious to

A mining track high on Great Dun Fell

follow throughout. A gentle rise is crossed at Tyne Head and a small notice announces the birth of the River South Tyne. Purists might like to chase this rivulet to its highest trickle. Newcastle and the North Sea are the Tyne's ultimate destiny, though they seem worlds apart from this vast moorland tract.

Continue along the track, which stays close to the infant Tyne as it gathers strength by picking up tributaries. The track crosses the river by bridge at a series of waterfalls caused by an outcrop of the Whin Sill. As the track climbs it crosses the line of the Great Sulphur Vein. Evidence of mining will have been noticed at a few points, the last being at Dorthgill, which overlooks the tiny hamlet of Tynehead - now in ruins.

If your non-walking motorist friend is a good navigator and timekeeper, then the walk can end with a joyful reunion a little way beyond Dorthgill. If not, then you might as well start plodding along the road to Garrigill while you ponder on what to do next.

East Fellside Section

The East Fellside is the most impressive flank of the North Pennines and home to that peculiar phenomenon - the Helm Wind. The highest Pennine summits are arranged in a formidable line, breached by only a handful of tracks and a single road. Some of the tracks are ancient, such as the Maiden Way. Others were once major thoroughfares which have been by-passed, as at Hartside. Mostly, they are old mining tracks - no longer required because the mines have been closed. One such track has been extended for grouse-shooting purposes, but the rest are slowly being reclaimed by the moors. For the most part, each of the walks feature an obvious line of ascent and descent, but route-finding errors on top could quickly lead into rough and remote country with few trodden routes.

WALK 7: BLACK FELL AND RENWICK

Have you ever wanted to park the car or get off the bus at around 2,000 feet (600 metres) and start walking? In the North Pennines that is easily arranged. The Hartside road isn't the highest road in these hills, but it does have a good car park and a cafe at over 1,900 feet (580 metres). The walk heads straight across the moors to Black Fell, then as height has been gained so effortlessly it is fairly easy to continue along to Watch Hill and Thack Moor. In mist and rain this would be something of a treadmill, so reserve it for fine weather. A long descent leads to the village of Renwick - then comes the catch - all the lost height has to be regained to return to the starting point.

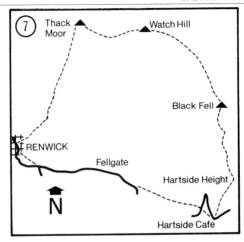

It is fully a 1,300 feet (400 metres) ascent to get back to the Hartside Cafe, but it's accomplished using roads and a fairly good track. You don't get "owt·fer nowt" and you don't get a leg up to a high level walk without paying for it somewhere else.

The Hartside Cafe stands proudly on a high gap between Alston and Penrith. It is England's highest cafe, though not particularly well-known for all that. It's only open in the summer months and winter visitors looking upon its boarded windows will swear that it's derelict. It has more character than the ugly shack on Snowdon's summit, and at least it's a traditional building - unlike the spaceship-like Ptarmigan Restaurant on Cairn Gorm. There's not as much hype about the place as there is about England's highest pubs - such as the Tan Hill Inn at 1,732 feet (528 metres) or the Cat and Fiddle Inn at 1,690 feet (515 metres). But if Hartside ever gets a licence... Well, we'll have to wait and see. In the meantime, snacks continue to be served to travellers on the Geordie short-cut to the Lake District.

The Hartside road is interesting because it is the only road breaching a thirty mile barrier of stern moorlands. All sorts of paths and tracks exist across the East Fellside flank of the North Pennines, but the Hartside road has emerged pre-eminent. Of course, it needed a helping hand. The London Lead Company struggled with inefficient transport routes from the lead mines of Alston Moor and finally decided that the badly eroded Hartside road needed attention. Around that time, John McAdam had settled in Penrith after writing a book called *The Present State of Road Making.* It was something of a best seller as books in that specialist field go and no doubt the "Quaker Company" had been influenced by it. McAdam surveyed the route and started reconstructing it in 1824. Typical "McAdamed" roads had sound foundations, lateral drainage ditches, a raised surface - and most importantly - a surface bound with clay to allow water to run off without carrying the roadstone with it. In later years a great deal of pitch and coal tar was used to bind the roadstone, giving us "Tar-McAdamed" roads. Thank you Mr McAdam, or should we say "Ta, Mac"?

If you've time to study the moorlands around the Hartside Cafe a number of old trackways will be noticed, many of which are being gobbled up by the advancing moor. Generally speaking, each successive construction cut out the steeper gradients of earlier routes. Winter has always been a problem at this height and the road is one of the first to be blocked by snow, along with Shap Fell and the Snake Pass. In such conditions, barriers are erected at Alston and Melmerby until the snowplough sets to work.

Renwick, in common with Croglin, also had a resident vampire. Apparently, the creature was disturbed when the old church was being demolished in 1845. A huge bat flew from the ruins and struck terror into the good folk of Renwick until it was nailed with a stave of rowan. Maybe there are others still undiscovered on the East Fellside?

THE ROUTE

Distance:	A moderate ten mile moorland walk with an easier finish.
Maps:	1:50,000 Landranger Sheet 86
	1:25,000 Pathfinder Sheets 568 & 569
Start/Finish:	The Hartside Cafe
Getting There:	The Hartside Cafe is on the highest part of the A686 between Alston and Penrith.
Parking:	At the Hartside Cafe and a nearby roadside quarry.

The Memorial Cairn on Watch Hill

Starting from the Hartside Cafe, walk a short way along the road in the Alston direction to reach a car park in a small quarry on the left. Cross a fence to get onto the moorland, then aim roughly northwards to follow a zig-zagging fence uphill. This line is replaced by a wall on Hartside Height. Continue uphill and a fence finally leads to the 2,179 feet (664 metres) trig point on Black Fell. Black because of the peat - which can sometimes be soft and wet too. The distance from the Hartside Cafe is two miles. There are three fences which meet on the summit: the one used on the walk so far; one to the right which heads across boggy ground to Tom Smith's Stone; and one to the left which is followed to continue the walk.

The fence runs downhill, then a wall carries on straight down Long Tongue - which is off our route. Turn right to follow a fence away from the wall, keeping roughly on the broad crest of the moorland. A junction of three walls is reached, with open country beyond rising to Watch Hill. The ascent of Watch Hill is plagued with a succession of false summits, but the gradients are easy. In poor visibility there are no aids to navigation, but the 1,975 feet (602 metres) summit bears a substantial ruined memorial cairn to someone surnamed Lowthian. There is little else on this broad, grassy, whaleback ridge. The summit is $1^3/_4$ miles from Black Fell and a walk of $1^1/_4$ miles leads to Thack Moor. Head straight towards Thack Moor, crossing a fence on the way. A wall leads to the summit trig point at 1,999 feet (609 metres). Being perched on the edge of this area of rolling moors, the view is good across the Vale of Eden.

It is tempting to follow a fence steeply downhill, but don't. Instead, let the eye be drawn to the left of the fence to pick up a green ribbon of a track far below. The track is aligned to a ruined wall and is easy to identify in clear weather. Head straight towards the track, passing close to an old coal mine on the way. The track leads further downhill and becomes enclosed by walls. Renwick is an attractive village about two miles down from Thack Moor. Turn left to follow the road into the village, but note that there is nothing on hand for a tired, hungry or thirsty walker. Continue straight through the village, following a road and track past the phone box. A signpost indicates Raven Bridge and a $^1/_4$ mile path leads across fields to join a minor road there.

Cross Raven Beck by the road bridge and note a "boundary perambulation" stone by the roadside. A minor road runs uphill for $1^1/_2$ miles, passing the farms of Haresceugh and Fellgate. Look out for a bridleway signpost on the left, which indicates Hartside. An obvious track runs past a ruin and out onto open moorland beyond. It must have been a major highway in its day, but the higher it climbs the more it has been reclaimed by the moorland. The main A686 is reached close to a low, solitary, white building. The main road attempts to ease the gradient by describing a wide zig-zag across the moorland slopes. Walkers can cut straight through the zig-zag by using a steep track which runs straight up to the Hartside Cafe. Food and drink are immediately to hand, with good views out over the Vale of Eden to the fells of the Lake District.

WALK 8: MELMERBY AND MELMERBY FELL

Melmerby Fell is high and wild, but easily approached by a good track from Melmerby. The track fades as it climbs, but is a faithful guide for most of the way. Actually, this route doesn't quite reach the summit of Melmerby Fell, but only a subsidiary shoulder called

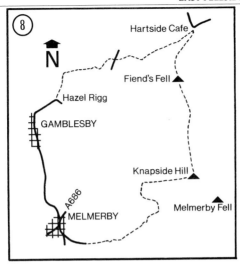

Knapside Hill. Ardent summit baggers can include the higher fell and retrace their steps to continue the route. After crossing Fiend's Fell the walk can be broken for a snack at the Hartside Cafe. An old road is used to descend to Gamblesby on the way back to Melmerby.

Fiend's Fell was the name of Cross Fell before some good missionary banished the fiends from that mighty summit. It seems that they only moved a few miles northwards. There must be a reason behind it all, or a good story at any rate, and I suspect that pagan veneration of spirits continued longer than is thought in this area.

Both Melmerby and Gamblesby are attractive, spacious villages, but Melmerby lies on the main road and has more to offer passing travellers in the way of food, drink and accommodation. Both are worth exploring while walking through, paying special attention to their fine, red sandstone buildings.

THE ROUTE

Distance:	A moderate 11 mile moorland walk with an easier finish.
Maps:	1:50,000 Landranger Sheets 86 & 91
	1:25,000 Pathfinder Sheets 569 & 578
Start/Finish:	Melmerby
Getting There:	Melmerby is on the A686 between Alston and Penrith. Minor roads on the East Fellside also reach it.
Parking:	Spaces around the village green.

Leave Melmerby by following the road signposted for Ousby. Turn left along a narrow road signposted for Melmerby Fell. As the road proceeds it becomes a gravel track, then a rather muddy track through a forest, then a fenced track running up towards the higher slopes. There is a gate which gives access to the open fellside, then the track swings to the left to go through another gate in the same fellside wall. The track continues to a series of limestone hummocks atop Melmerby Low Scar. Take a break here to study the view down to the village and across the Vale of Eden. As the track rises, it forsakes the limestone pastures for the wiry moorland grasses and zig-zags further uphill. A gate is passed through close to a vehicle of indeterminate make which was brought to this height before giving up the ghost.

The scene ahead is of a vast boulderfield. The track moves easily through it using an excavated hollow-way. Once through the boulderfield, look eastwards to pick out a prominent cairn on the horizon and head across pathless country to climb to it. The cairn stands on Knapside Hill at 2,247 feet (685 metres) about 3½ miles up from Melmerby. This is the shoulder of Melmerby Fell and the actual summit can be reached in a simple ½ mile ascent, but Knapside Hill is a finer situation. There is quite a good view over Alston Moor, the East Fellside and the Vale of Eden.

Head northwards for 1½ miles to continue over Little Knapside Hill to reach Fiend's Fell. There is no path, the way can be wet and boggy, and there is the odd fence to cross. Fiend's Fell is an obvious, broad, pudding of a hill capped by a trig point at 2,082 feet (634 metres). It could be passed unknowingly in mist, but the A686 would be reached at some point. A grassy track leads down from

Fiend's Fell to the Hartside Cafe. Food and drink are on hand there at over 1,900 feet (580 metres). The place is a haven in bad weather, but note that it is closed in the winter months.

If the cafe isn't required, then turn left just before reaching a power line. Look across the moorland slopes to discern the line of a rushy shelf - probably once a major highway. This line is wet and boggy and it is better to remain upslope of it to stay dry-shod. The track becomes better at Twotop Hill about a mile from Hartside. It descend more steeply, then reaches the access road for an ugly mast. Follow the access road down to the A686 and cross straight over. A walled track continues downhill for 1¹/₄ miles, twisting and turning until it reaches a minor road at Hazel Rigg. Turn right to follow this road, then walk straight through a crossroads to enter the village of Gamblesby. Colourful agricultural implements are displayed by the roadside. A small church and pub are worth investigating. Melmerby lies 1¹/₄ miles further along the minor road. The Post Haste Cafe, Village Bakery and Shepherd's Inn jointly rise to satisfy hunger or thirst generated on the walk. A few fine, red sandstone buildings are worth studying before leaving.

WALK 9: THE MAIDEN WAY

The Maiden Way is a high-level Roman road which offers a fairly straightforward walk from Alston Moor to the East Fellside. Straight is the operative word, as with most Roman roads, and this poses a logistical problem. It is handy for the walker to be dropped off at the start, on the A686, and collected at the end, which is the village of Kirkland. There is public transport in the area, but it is very patchy. As a walk, the Maiden Way also has some patchy sections, but with care there should be no problem identifying the route and the route description notes handy features to look for.

The Maiden Way is the second highest Roman road in Britain - the highest of all being High Street in the Lake District. The Romans surrounded the North Pennines with some major highways, then for some reason cut a line from a fort at Kirkby Thore straight to Hadrian's Wall. It seems safe to assume that they were after lead, but there is no real evidence of their workings. It also seems safe to assume that Whitley Castle was sited to control the industry in the Alston Moor region. There are many things we don't know. We don't know if the Romans had names for their roads. *Maydengathe* was the name of the route in an abbey record of 1179. When Reginald Bainbrigg was headmaster of Appleby Grammar School he fed William Camden with information for his "Brittanica" which was published in 1586. Bainbrigg spoke of a fort at Greenhead and said that, "from there goeth a street called Mayden Way, which is paved with stones throughout the moors, about some forty miles in length, to Mayden Castle upon Stainemoor." Walkers interested in Roman engineering will delight to find some perfect stretches of the Maiden Way, but some parts are buried beneath the moors and the approach to Melmerby Shop has been resurfaced.

Melmerby Shop is something to bear in mind in case of foul weather. This is a little cottage which keeps out of sight of the Maiden Way, but is served by a short track from it. The building was gradually falling into disrepair until outdoor enthusiasts rescued it and patched it up with help from the owner. A log book records the comings and goings of wanderers and one note begs, "Don't tell the Mountain Bothies Association." For some reason the Ordnance Survey deleted it from their maps, but the grid reference

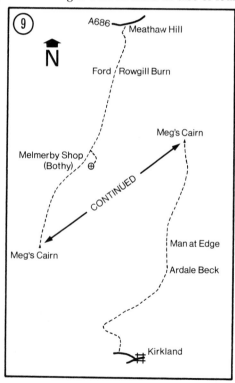

is 668392.

Long distance walkers might be pondering on Reginald Bainbrigg's statement about the Maiden Way being forty miles long. Quite honestly, it doesn't make a particularly good long walk. The best section is the one offered here. It is possible to link minor roads and footpaths in South Tynedale to get from Greenhead to Whitley Castle. It is possible to trace the line of the Maiden Way over to Meathaw Hill. The route as described below conveys walkers over to Kirkland. The continuation to Kirkby Thore has been obliterated by agriculture. The rest of the line to Stainmore has largely been overlain by the busy A66 and is too dangerous for walkers. It is possible to see "Mayden Castle upon Stainemoor" on Walk 15, which is the only other enjoyable part of the Maiden Way.

Kirkland is a small village with nothing to offer the walker but a peep at its little church. The church has been restored and has no interesting relics, which is a pity as its list of rectors stretches as far back as 1163. Maps also note the "Hanging Gardens of Mark Anthony" near Kirkland. Don't bother rushing to see this feature. Whoever thought up such a grand name for a bit of wrinkled ground was ·obviously an incurable romantic. Save all your imagination for the walk - following the footsteps of enlightened engineers who were undeterred by the formidable flank of the East Fellside.

THE ROUTE

Distance:	A moderate seven mile moorland walk on a fairly clear track.
Maps:	1:50,000 Landranger Sheets 86 & 91
	1:25,000 Pathfinder Sheets 569 & 578
Start:	Meathaw Hill
Finish:	Kirkland
Getting There:	Meathaw Hill is on the A686 between Alston and Hartside.
	Kirkland is reached via Kirkby Thore or Langwathby.
Parking:	Limited at Meathaw Hill. More space at Kirkland.

The walk starts where a small plantation runs downhill from the A686 road - about four miles up from Alston and two miles down from the Hartside Cafe. A walled track runs downhill alongside the plantation. Walk down the track, then go through a gate on the left and continue downhill to Rowgill Burn. The burn has to be forded before picking up an obvious track across the moors. In wet weather, this means wet feet - only $1/2$ mile into the walk. The track, which overlies the Maiden Way, runs straight up the moorland slope for $1^1/4$ miles, then executes a most un-Roman sharp left turn. Actually, what happens is that the Maiden Way is still running uphill, though much less definitely. The left turning leads to Melmerby Shop, which is a small bothy out of sight of the Maiden Way, but handy in case of foul weather. Its grid reference is 668392.

The course of the Maiden Way is south-westwards and the old road is distinguished from the surrounding moorlands by its lighter vegetation. Sometimes the way is perfectly clear - being a well banked, wide, raised track with a stony surface. At other times it is less clear, sunken and boggy. It is $1^1/2$ miles from the bothy to Meg's Cairn at around 2,200 feet (670 metres). This is the highest part of the Maiden Way. Summit baggers might well be drawn to include the top of Melmerby Fell, but the old Roman road is more absorbing and the bouldery surroundings are better than the blank fell-top.

The Maiden Way makes a little twist and turn to negotiate a bouldery edge before running directly southwards. The route becomes aligned to a wall and goes through the first gate. After going through two more gates on an obvious downhill run a well-defined track branches to the right across the flank of Muska Hill. This is not the Maiden Way, but it does offer a good route straight down to Ousby Row in bad weather. The Maiden Way actually continues less distinctly along a high terrace. Take care not to be deflected left to a solitary lime kiln, but continue along an improving track to descend to Man at Edge. The "Man" is a small mine building $1^1/2$ miles down from Meg's Cairn. Note the half-buried rails running downhill.

Kirkland lies $2^1/4$ miles roughly southwards from Man at Edge, but the line of the Maiden Way is unclear. If it was ever properly delineated, then it has been obliterated. Descend steeply straight into Ardale. Cross Ardale Beck by the first footbridge and climb up the slight slope beyond. A vague footpath crosses rough pasture and keeps to the left of a wooded gill. Anyone swinging too far left from this line will reach Bank Hall farm, which doesn't really matter, but the track through the farmyard isn't a right of way. On the correct course, turn left when a track is reached and follow this to the access road from Bank Hall Farm. The access road joins a minor road and a final left turn leads straight to the little church at Kirkland - dedicated to St. Lawrence. Provided that someone is waiting to collect you with a car, the walk is over. If not, then the only bus service is the voluntary Fellrunner Community Minibus. If neither option is available, it's a long walk to the main road.

WALK 10: BLENCARN AND CROSS FELL

The vast majority of walkers who visit Cross Fell are Pennine Wayfarers tackling the difficult 16 miles from Dufton to Garrigill (or 20 miles to Alston if they are hostelling). The only trouble with the Pennine Way is that it climbs Cross Fell from the shoulders of other fells. The walk from Blencarn deals with Cross Fell purely for its own sake, savouring every bit of its great height and experiencing something of its vastness. Blencarn is a quiet village set around a green. It seems to be surrounded by fields, but a curious corridor of rough pasture connects it to the flank of Cross Fell. This corridor will have been left unenclosed to allow sheep and cattle to be brought straight from the fellside to the heart of the village. An old trackway continues uphill towards Tees Head. There is evidence to show that this was used by pack-horse traffic, but it has long been neglected and is difficult to trace in places. The Pennine Way is used to cross the summit plateau. The descent is accomplished by using the old "Corpse Road" linking Garrigill to Kirkland.

Cross Fell is the highest of all the Pennine fells and the highest bit of English ground outside of the Lake District. It all depends on how you arrange your tables of height, but Cross Fell lies between Great Gable and Pillar in order of altitude and therefore gains itself a place in England's Top Ten Tops, if you like.

If you look in bothy books and church visitor books in the area, walkers sometimes write "Cross Fell *was* cross". It used to be called Fiend's Fell and that name was recorded in 1340 and 1479. When William Camden passed through Eden gathering information for his book *Brittanica*, published in 1586, he wrote that mass had been

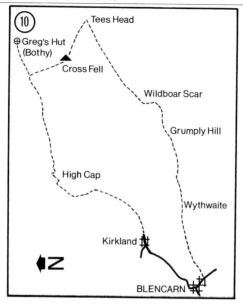

said on the summit and a cross planted to banish the fiends. St. Paulinus of York and St. Augustine of Canterbury have both been credited with the exorcism, but the timing of the change of name rules out both. Could this be a muddled folk-memory? Perhaps - just perhaps - an Augustinian from Carlisle, Paulinus by name, did the good deed around 1500. Whatever the truth, the fiends don't seem to have entirely departed as there is a Fiend's Fell a few miles to the north-west.

Corpse Roads are surrounded by a curious mythology, but after stripping them down they turn out to be no more than common-or-garden links between two settlements. Centuries ago, if one village had a church and a consecrated burial ground, and another hadn't, then any bodies for burial had to be packed over the fells just like any other goods for shipment. If anyone died in winter - tough - they were put into "cold storage" until the spring thaw allowed traffic to move once more. The Corpse Road between Garrigill and Kirkland runs to 2,600 feet (790 metres) and is therefore the highest of its kind.

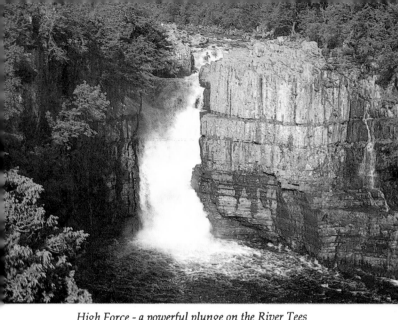

High Force - a powerful plunge on the River Tees

Redgate Head and the old line above Rookhope

Cross Fell also holds the English record for snow cover into the month of July. There is a story told of Garrigill folk setting out for a burial in spring, only to be overtaken by a blizzard on the fell. Unceremonially ditching their deceased, they hurried back to Garrigill and waited for better conditions. Another expedition was mounted, but again bad weather forced a retreat. This time, however, they managed to get the corpse back to Garrigill. The bishop was duly informed of the difficulties and Garrigill was granted its own consecrated burial plot. Anyone delving deeply into this story will find all sorts of inconsistencies, but it serves to illustrate that Cross Fell, its remoteness and its fickle weather should be treated with care and respect. In good weather, this is one of the finest walks in the North Pennines - a fine challenge abounding in interest.

THE ROUTE

Distance: A difficult 11 mile fellwalk, mostly on good paths.
Maps: 1:50,000 Landranger Sheet 91
                  1:25,000 Pathfinder Sheet 578
Start/Finish: Blencarn
Getting There: Blencarn can be reached via minor roads from
                  Kirkby Thore and Langwathby.
Parking: Spaces around the village green.

Start near the Cross Keys Farm in Blencarn, where a bridleway sign points towards Cross Fell. All around Blencarn are green fields, but the bridleway is routed along a rough corridor more akin to the higher moorlands. After a mile the farmhouse of Wythwaite is passed and the route soon moves into open country. A grassy track on the side of Grumply Hill runs uphill parallel to a small beck. A narrow track cuts across a steeper fellside and leads to the top of Wildboar Scar. The distance from Blencarn is 2³/₄ miles and clear weather is an advantage on the next 1¹/₂ miles to Tees Head. There is a path running roughly north-westwards, but it is vague in places. There are a few small cairns, an upright stone pillar and some sections which have been artificially banked with stones for pack-horse use, but the way has largely fallen into disrepair. Look out for fell ponies on the ascent, possibly descended from stock which once used the route.

Greg's Hut - a useful bothy high on Cross Fell

Tees Head is a disappointment for those who know the mighty River Tees and its roaring cataracts. This is just a peaty gap like any other in the Pennines. All you can hope to do is to gaze eastwards and imagine the course of the river. The Pennine Way is followed over Cross Fell by turning left and walking steeply uphill. A watercourse runs over the path and the way is badly overtrodden. The higher parts of the fell seem largely immune to booted feet. Cross Fell's wide, oval plateau is vegetated with short turf and offers a fine high-level campsite. Summit structures include a trig point at 2,970 feet (893 metres), a cross-shelter, one large cairn and a number of smaller ones. As for the view, this is best observed from the edges of the plateau, which means quite a long walk to take it all in. The Vale of Eden spreads out a vast patchwork towards the serrated skyline of Lakeland Fells. A few hills can be seen in the Southern Uplands of Scotland, with the Cheviots forming a conspicuous group. Northern parts of the Yorkshire Dales can be seen, with the rest of the vista taken up by rolling heathery heights from all parts of the North Pennines. On a very clear day a small scale map helps the identification of distant features.

Use the Pennine Way to leave the summit. This is poorly defined and picks its way down a bouldery slope to reach a large cairn on a good track. Pennine Wayfarers turn right to reach Garrigill, and anyone who needs an emergency shelter from the elements should go that way for ½ mile to reach Greg's Hut. The route to Blencarn, however, is leftwards at the large cairn. A wet and stony track crosses the shoulder of Cross Fell at 2,600 feet (790 metres). The upper section is rather patchy, but it gains a better surface on the long descent when it encounters a colliery track. A steep fellside below High Cap is negotiated by zig-zags. The gradient eases as the lower slopes are reached and a track finally follows Kirkland Beck through Kirkland. The village is about 4½ miles down from Cross Fell's summit. There is nothing on offer for a tired and hungry walker, but the little church of St. Lawrence is mildly interesting. It has no ancient relics, but a list of rectors dates as far back as 1163. Blencarn is an easy mile away by road and the village has a little more to offer in the way of facilities.

WALK 11: DUFTON AND HIGH CUP

Most day-walkers making a visit to High Cup simply follow the Pennine Way from Dufton and retrace their steps later. This is reasonable for anyone pushed for time, but it doesn't display High Cup to its best advantage. Pennine Wayfarers trek in from Langdon Beck and suddenly stumble upon High Cup without any build-up. This is the way it should be seen, but day-walkers who have to return to Langdon Beck for their cars will find it a punishing walk. The route offered here tries a different tactic - climbing to the high moors by a route which is itself interesting, seeking out the best approach to High Cup, then returning to Dufton via the Pennine Way. Great Rundale is used as a way to the vast moorlands and it has a good, clear track all the way. After toying with the wilderness for a couple of miles, High Cup is approached and appreciated the same way Pennine Wayfarers manage it. A well-blazed path and track leave for a fairly quick return to Dufton.

The Whin Sill is present along the length of the East Fellside flank of the North Pennines. It seldom goes unnoticed, but the landforms it produces vary enormously. Most of the time it outcrops as a rugged scar, or occurs as a bouldery slope. Sometimes it is entirely grass-grown. In the valleys it tends to show as a resistant rim. At High Cup the Whin Sill produces the most spectacular dale-head in the North Pennines. The horizontal nature of the sill is apparent as its weather-resistant edge stands out starkly to form a colonaded rim around the edges.

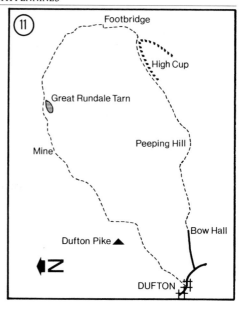

The slopes above seem to fall back as if in awe, while the steep-sided dale itself is empty, silent, rock-strewn and primeval. High Cup is its real name, though many people call it High Cup Nick. The nick is a cleft cut in the rocky rim. Another little feature is a tall column known as Nichol's Chair. Nichol was a cobbler from Dufton who scaled the column and soled and heeled a pair of boots on top. The Pennine Way is routed along the break of slope along the edge of High Cup. Parts of the path have been worn down to bedrock and look deceptively as if they have been paved. A narrow section is appropriately named the Narrowgate.

Dufton is a pleasant red sandstone village set around a large green. It has become an important staging post on the Pennine Way, lying between two particularly wild sections. There is a Youth Hostel, pub and shop. The Parish Church isn't in the village, but stands half way to Knock. Although a fairly recent structure, its list of rectors dates back to 1293. The whole area was a Norman hunting forest and remained largely unsettled. Dufton Hall dates from the 16th Century and other buildings have 17th Century dates. Mining didn't really take off until the 18th Century. Some say that the London Lead Company built Dufton, but this is obviously untrue. They did, however, extend and re-order the village. The sandstone fountain on the green was provided by the "Quaker Company".

Lead mining ceased in Great Rundale around 1900, but the mine remained open for the extraction of barytes until 1924. The spoil heaps have been worked in recent years for barytes and some limited underground work has been accomplished. The access track has been rather brutally renovated to accommodate vehicles and some noisy machinery has been installed. Maps haven't yet caught up with the fact that the mining track has been extended to allow shooting parties to reach Great Rundale Tarn.

THE ROUTE

Distance: A moderate ten mile moorland walk on good tracks and paths.
Maps: 1:50,000 Landranger Sheet 91
               1:25,000 Outdoor Leisure Sheet 31
Start/Finish: Dufton
Getting There: Dufton is most easily reached by following minor roads from Appleby, itself on the A66.
Parking: Spaces around the village green.

Leave Dufton via Dufton Hall, where a bridleway sign indicates High Scald Fell. A narrow track crosses a couple of small becks, then runs uphill past Pusgill House. This is no place to meet a vehicle, but the track becomes wider at higher levels and it is easier to step to one side. The track sneaks behind the massive cone of Dufton Pike to enter Great Rundale. The surroundings are quite rugged, with steep rock walls enclosing the dale. The track becomes rather stony where it has been bulldozed wider for vehicles. An old mining site is reached which has been revitalised for the extraction of barytes. Although the map doesn't yet admit it, the track has been extended a further 1/2 mile for shooting purposes. Easy walking ends some 3 1/2 miles up from Dufton at about 2,200 feet (670 metres). There is an old shelter hut here which overlooks Great Rundale Tarn. It is as well to note that Great Rundale Tarn doesn't in fact drain into Great Rundale, but feeds Maize beck and ultimately reaches the North Sea. Notice also how suddenly the wilderness becomes apparent at this point.

Locate the outlet of Great Rundale Tarn and walk downstream. There are a number of shooting butts on the moorland and progress may be barred when shooting is taking place. It is generally best to keep to the northern bank of the beck to descend. This is the roughest part of the route and after 1¹/₂ miles the deep, dark gorge confining Maize Beck is reached. Scramblers drawn to the innards should take care as parts are unstable. The rock walls hold a few plants which are unusual and cannot be grazed by sheep. Trees also gain a roothold and include hornbeam.

At the footbridge, it is a good idea to check on the direction as this area is rather broad and flat and could be especially confusing in mist. Walk roughly southwards from the footbridge, then drift more south-westwards. On this course, High Cup will suddenly break upon the scene and if the distance is blessed with a view to the fells of the Lake District, then this is an added bonus. The colonaded rim seems to embrace the view and stony slopes fall steeply to a green carpeted floor. Fell ponies might be seen.

Leave by following the Pennine Way along the northern rim. This is clearly trodden and presents no problems. Look out for the column known as Nichol's Chair, take a drink from the clear spring of Hannah's Well, then tread along the rocky Narrowgate path. There is sustained interest throughout, then the special features become rather less, the slopes fall back more gently and High Cup gradually becomes like most other North Pennine dales. The Pennine Way moves further downhill, remaining an obvious path, until it is swallowed between enclosing walls. As the track runs downhill it becomes surfaced with tarmac. Turn right at the very end to return to the centre of Dufton. A visit to the pub or a wander through the woods of Dufton Gill makes a pleasant end to the day's walking. If there are any Pennine Wayfarers about, notice how much more weary they seem.

Warcop Range Section

WALK 12: Murton, Murton Fell and Scordale
WALK 13: Hilton and Tinside Rigg
WALK 14: Mickle Fell

These three walks have peculiar problems of access and all lie in the vast Warcop Training Range. Public access is permitted during clear periods - usually Mondays - and these can be checked by phoning **Brough 661** and asking for the **Range Officers' Department.** The walk from Murton is only half in the Danger Area and can be adapted even when firing is in progress. Walk 13 is entirely within the Danger Area and stray shells are very evident. The walk up Mickle Fell is remote from the Primary Impact Area, but has other access problems which are unresolved. All three walks are "at your own risk" as dozens of warning signs proclaim. It all sounds rather grim, but this area is too good to be omitted entirely. In all other respects, this is a continuation of the East Fellside section.

WALK 12: MURTON, MURTON FELL AND SCORDALE

Murton Fell has two very gentle swellings which pass for its summits. This is useful because one of the summits is in the Danger Area of the Warcop Training Range and the other isn't. Thus, it is possible to walk up Murton Fell whatever the condition of the range. To continue the route over Murton Fell to reach Scordale, walkers should check that there is no firing. The walk uses a good track to reach Murton Pike and Murton Fell, but it gradually deteriorates and Murton Fell can be an awkward place for navigation in mist. The descent via Scordale uses a good path and track, with field paths used to effect a link between Hilton and Murton to end the walk.

Scordale, which is within the Warcop Training Range, has an interesting mining site which was developed by the London Lead

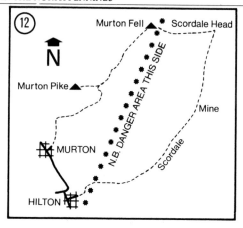

Company. A huddle of ruins high up the dale housed water-powered ore-crushers and a smelt mill. A long fellside flue carried toxic fumes away from the site and allowed the condensation of substances which would otherwise have been lost. The sides of Scordale are pock-marked with holes and scars, but these do not detract from the grandeur of the place. Steep, rocky walls enclose the dale and give it an air of secrecy. Further down-dale is Lowfield Hush, where dammed water was released to scour away the sub-soil and reveal any traces of mineral veins. The lowest building in the dale was constructed as a smelt mill, but later served as a crushing mill for barytes. The "Quaker Company" gave their most loyal workers small allotments in the lower dale. The company held the lease on the Scordale mines until the 1880s, but when lead mining ceased the deposits of barytes continued to be worked until the 1950s. Anyone wondering why the mining ruins should be in such an advanced state of decay should realise that the army knocked them about a bit.

What the inhabitants of Murton and Hilton think of the Warcop Training Range is nobody's business, but discreet enquiries will reveal a fund of stories. A lot of haggling goes on about night firing. Much of the higher land is used for sheep grazing and the commoners negotiate with the army authorities for clear periods of several days for gathering the flocks. Again, by checking with the Range Officer's Department walkers could take advantage of several days without firing to complete their walks.

Murton and Hilton are typical East Fellside settlements, occupying the final break of slope between the heights and the lower pastures. Hilton has a pub and post office, while Murton has even less than that in the way of facilities. Water seems to have been a problem in the past, with the main becks being polluted by lead mining. Murton's supply comes from a fellside tank, while Hilton's village street still features old, stone water points from which the villagers used to draw their supplies. Brackenber Moor offers a fine approach to the area - part sheep grazing and part golf course - with a fine view of the East Fellside as far as Cross Fell.

THE ROUTE

Distance:	A moderate nine mile moorland walk with some good tracks. (Six miles if returning directly to Murton from Murton Fell)
Maps:	1:50,000 Landranger Sheet 91
	1:25,000 Outdoor Leisure Sheet 31
Start/Finish:	Murton
Getting There:	Murton is most easily reached by following minor roads from Appleby, itself on the A66.
Parking:	At a green with immediate access to the fellside.

Starting from a green at Murton, go through a gate giving access to the fellside. An obvious track runs up the flank of Murton Pike - visible from afar in this area. The track twists and turns uphill until it is well behind the summit of Murton Pike. At this point, branch off leftwards and climb the remaining distance to the trig point at 1,949 feet (594 metres). Almost 1³/₄ miles have been walked from Murton, yet the village is only a mile away. There is a good view over the Vale of Eden and along the East Fellside. The Lakeland Fells, Howgill Fells and part of the Yorkshire Dales feature well.

Retrace steps to the main track and continue uphill towards Murton Fell. The way forward crosses a stony waste, but the gradient is easy throughout. The track expires, but continue walking uphill in the same direction. Find any point which looks as if it might

Murton Pike rises outside the 'Danger Area'

be the actual summit of Murton Fell, around 2,200 feet (670 metres). There are actually two slight swellings which could be called the top, but there is an important difference - one is outside of the Warcop Training Range and the other inside. If firing is taking place on the range, then this is as far as we should come. Turn around and walk back down to Murton. If there is no firing, then continue as follows.

Walk past the warning notices to gain the other summit of Murton Fell, at 2,207 feet (673 metres). Walk eastwards to locate Scordale Head. This is a boggy gap between Murton Fell and Little Fell, about 1/2 mile down from the summit of Murton Fell. Be sure to turn right to walk down into Scordale as the other direction is a remote wilderness. At first Scordale is exceedingly narrow and flanked by steep, grassy slopes. The dale widens later and becomes fringed with attractively rugged cliffs. A number of ruined buildings come into view - the remains of the old lead mine. Although this is a scene of industrial decay, there is still a wild feel about the place. Study the outlines of the buildings and trace the lines of old structures, but keep well clear as there are dangerous holes and some walls are becoming rather tottery. The mine is about a mile down Scordale and another two miles downhill on the old track leads to Hilton. The track stays close to Scordale Beck and the side-stream of Swindale Beck has to be forded. The village is finally reached by making a sharp left turn immediately followed by a right turn. The Danger Area of the Warcop Training Range is left behind here.

Go straight down through Hilton, admiring the red sandstone buildings and old, stone water points. If a pub is required, then turn left at the phone box. If not, then turn right and walk to a nearby road junction. Just beside a signpost at the junction is a small stile. This gives access to a field path which leads straight towards Murton. It rejoins the road between two chapels - one in use and the other converted to a dwelling. Turn left to walk into Murton, then right to reach the parking space on the high green.

WALK 13: HILTON AND TINSIDE RIGG

Here's a walk through the heart of the Warcop Training Range, following bridleways, footpaths and roads through the Primary Impact Area itself. Admittedly, this walk isn't for the faint-hearted and there are literally dozens of unexploded shells lying on the ground in certain areas. Most shelling takes place from the lower ground and the western flank of Roman Fell is supposed to take the punishment. Some shells, however, seem to go over the top or around the sides. A significant number don't seem to explode - perhaps the army should return them to the manufacturer! It is unwise for walkers to tamper with anything odd they find and it is a criminal offence to remove anything. The danger to life and limb is obvious and stories of children burning specimens in dustbins to see if they explode are frightening. Superstitious walkers might bear in mind that the plan of this guide was already far advanced before it was realised that this walk was number 13!

The main reason for offering a walk in this area is not to keep the rights of way open, nor for sheer bloody-mindedness, but because the area itself is worth seeing. Swindale is a secret dale which runs at right-angles to all other East Fellside dales. It has to be entered to be properly appreciated. Roman Fell has an aggressive face which

One of the many unexploded shells lying around on the Warcop Range

is best studied at close quarters. From Tinside Rigg it is possible to experience the sheer scale and desolation of Little Fell - surely the most inappropriate name for this huge, sprawling wilderness. The limestone outcrop of Middle Fell can be seen from the A66, but from above it has a completely different aspect. The lower slopes, true, don't have much scenic merit, but if you've never walked through an artillery range before you might be interested at what goes on there. The route offered is entirely on rights of way so that, firing permitting, there can be no question of your right to walk there.

The ascent from Hilton is via Scordale, which features a good, clear track. The side-dale of Swindale has a fairly good track which quickly gains height, but it disappears in tricky country. In clear weather, there should be no problem navigating over Tinside Rigg and descending to Dogber Tarn, but there is no trodden path and the public bridleway can only be followed on an approximate course. The descent from Dogber Tarn to the A66 is quite clear and the return to Hilton is by road. It's a long walk, but not unduly difficult in good weather. The main thing is to keep an eye on the route and keep an eye open for odd shells lying around. In the meantime, enjoy the scenery and old mining sites.

Hilton is a quiet little village - when firing isn't in progress - and has a number of fine red sandstone buildings. There is a pub and post office, which might prove useful for a drink and a bite to eat. The village street still features old, stone water points from which the villagers used to draw their supplies. Brackenber Moor offers a fine approach to the area - part sheep grazing and part golf course - with a fine view of the East Fellside as far as Cross Fell.

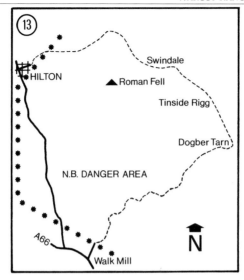

THE ROUTE

Distance:	A moderate 11 mile fellwalk, mostly on good tracks.
Maps:	1:50,000 Landranger Sheet 91
	1:25,000 Outdoor Leisure Sheet 31 &
	Pathfinder Sheet 597
Start/Finish:	Hilton
Getting There:	Hilton is most easily reached by minor roads from the A66 near Appleby or Brough.
Parking:	Small spaces in the village. Ask permission if in doubt.

Start in Hilton and follow the road uphill from the phone box. This runs straight out of the village as a gravel track, then descends to Scordale Beck. A whole series of brightly coloured signs stand sentinel by a gate. It all seems very forbidding, but provided there is no firing you are at liberty to proceed. With half an hour to spare you could read all the regulations pertaining to the range, but life is too short and the wilderness beckons.

Continue along the gravel track close to the beck. After more than a mile Swindale Beck flows across the track and a little care is needed to avoid wet feet when it is in spate. Turn right immediately after the ford to enter Swindale. Height is gained by using an old track on the fellside which has deteriorated into a boggy groove lined with stones. Don't be dismayed at this line, as it gets much better with height and becomes a fine, grassy track which leads effortlessly onwards. Views back down the dale allow a little peep out towards the fells of the Lake District.

After a mile the path becomes rather vague, but on a clear day there should be no problem continuing the walk. Simply head for the highest part of the dale-head, which is called Tinside Rigg. To mark progress towards this point, look out for a small, derelict mining site above a limestone ravine, then a ruined sheepfold at a higher level. These features occur on the way to Tinside Rigg, as do a number of unexploded shells, so watch your feet. Tinside Rigg is flanked by boggy ground, but is quite firm itself. A tremendous panorama is available which reaches from Skiddaw to Shap Fell, taking in the Lakeland Fells. The Howgill Fells and Yorkshire Dales lead the eye round to the Stainmore wastes. Rising above Tinside Rigg is the vast, open wilderness of Little Fell.

The ground beyond Tinside Rigg is roughly vegetated. The best means of progress is to walk along an exposed rib of rock to get downhill. Dogber Tarn comes into view and the best way down is simply to head straight for it. Beware more unexploded shells on the way. Follow the outflowing beck from Dogber Tarn to start the next stage of the descent. This crosses a wide track, but continue down into a dry valley. A number of old pathways exist as grooves down the valley. Again, there are numerous unexploded shells. Continue downhill and gradually drift away from the beck as it reappears.

Turn right along the first definite track encountered on the lower slopes. This twists and turns, but gradually leads down towards the A66. The Warcop Training Range is left behind shortly before a strip of tarmac leads down to the A66. There is probably more to fear from oncoming traffic on this road than on the firing range. Walkers will be glad to turn right at a sign for the ABC Ranges. A rather dull road walk of nearly three miles returns to Hilton. The Cross Keys pub is available on entering the village and there may be time for a quiet drink and a chance to relax after constantly trying to avoid stepping on unexploded shells. One day the army will vacate the area and when all the junk has been cleared away it can take its place alongside other interesting parts of the East Fellside.

WALK 14: MICKLE FELL

Mickle Fell has been included in this section simply because it is within the designated Danger Area of the Warcop Training Range. At such a distance from the Primary Impact Area the danger from a stray shell must be negligible. My own wanderings over the years have revealed no unexploded shells. Both shepherds and seasoned wilderness walkers have scoffed at any suggestion of danger during firing. A couple of Youth Hostel wardens once cynically remarked that they considered the Danger Area was artificially extended over Mickle Fell to deter visitors. All this is of course a matter of opinion and walkers will have to satisfy themselves of the likelihood of any danger. The Range Officers' Department will be pleased to advise walkers of clear periods, but they aren't in a position to give walkers permission to make an ascent of Mickle Fell.

There is another problem with routes. The fell is part of the vast Upper Teesdale National Nature Reserve. They have a simple policy on access - stick to the rights of way. As there aren't any, walkers quickly reach a full stop. The nearest rights of way are distant and using them as a stepping stone to the summit makes for a long day's walk. The Nature Conservancy only manage the area in respect of its remarkable plant life - they don't own it.

The owners manage the area for grouse shooting and don't allow access on the grounds that it will disturb the grouse. Presumably artillery bombardment doesn't disturb the grouse? The Rambler's Association has been pressing for access to Mickle Fell for years, without making any headway. They finally had to use their ultimate weapon - the Mass Trespass. About seventy ramblers reached the summit after a rally in October 1986.

Getting permission to climb Mickle Fell is practically impossible, yet more and more people are claiming to have made the ascent. I'm offering a route I've used before in another book, but must point out that walkers will have to decide for themselves if they are going to

79

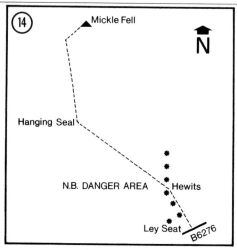

use the route. I give the route for the following reasons: it is short; easy; far away from shooting butts; doesn't cover any sensitive plant sites; is clearly marked on the ground; is out of sight of anyone who would worry about walkers being there in the first place; and it has a novelty "ascent by numbers" set of boundary stones. Maybe it's the best of a bad job, but I think it is a reasonable route for walkers until there is a thaw in the access position.

Meanwhile, what of Mickle Fell itself? Its name points to it being a "big" fell, but it is also a proudly remote part of the North Pennines. It used to be the highest point in Yorkshire, until boundary realignments made it the highest point in Durham. Someone thought enough of the fell to crown it with a huge stone cairn. The North Pennines would be a poorer place without Mickle Fell and a guidebook omitting it would only be half a guidebook to the area. It's there in all its supreme wilderness if you want it, but pick a reasonable day for the ascent and avoid wandering on its trackless wastes in poor visibility. I was once thrashed off the fell by rain, sleet and hail and retreated to a farmhouse. When the farmer heard where I'd been he remarked "By, she'd be cold up there." I wasn't sure who "she" was meant to be - the weather or Mickle Fell - but I'd have described both as aggressively masculine.

THE ROUTE

Distance: A difficult seven mile moorland walk without any paths.

Maps: 1:50,000 Landranger Sheets 91 or 92
1:25,000 Outdoor Leisure Sheet 31

Start/Finish: Ley Seat.

Getting There: Ley Seat is on the B6276 between Brough and Middleton-in-Teesdale, on the Cumbria and Durham boundary.

Parking: Small space by the roadside.

Start on the B6276 road at the cattle grid on the Cumbria and Durham boundary. The key to the ascent of Mickle Fell from this point is to follow the county boundary roughly north-west and later northwards to reach the summit. Against the wall near the cattle grid is a boundary stone deeply inscribed with the number 46. Follow the wall uphill at first, but when it turns sharply left continue along the line of a ruined fence. Keep an eye on the boundary stones, which appear in ascending numerical order, though not all are present. Number 54 stands on the shoulder of Hewits, where the fence turns slightly to the left. The walk is already within the Danger Area of the Warcop Training Range. The line of warning signs can be seen marching across the moors, though the Primary Impact Area is distant.

A descent leads to Connypot Beck, which must be forded. This is the widest and deepest of a number of becks which have to be forded. If Connypot Beck poses no problems, neither will the rest. They all merge to form the River Lune further eastwards. Continue along the fence-line to reach boundary stone number 70 at Hanging Seal. Several fences join at this point, which marks the junction of five parishes (why should they meet in such a desolate spot?). A fairly new fence heads roughly northwards, uphill at an easy gradient. At the foot of a steeper slope is a notice marking the boundary of the Upper Teesdale National Nature Reserve - so they must expect someone to come this way. Follow the fence steeply uphill to reach a more level area. Turn right, away from the fence, to reach the huge summit cairn on Mickle Fell.

Some 3$^{1}/_{2}$ miles have been walked to reach the 2,591 feet (790 metres) summit. The view takes in seemingly endless rolling moorlands and is a fine place to study the North Pennine wilderness. Further afield there are views into the Lake District and Yorkshire Dales. There are many ways of leaving the summit, but they all involve long and difficult walks. The ascent route is difficult enough, but also the easiest way up. The quickest and easiest way down is to reverse the same route. Walk back to the fence and be sure to turn left to go downhill. Heading down to Maize Beck is asking for trouble as the only real way to continue a walk would involve fording the beck at some point.

Stainmore Section

Stainmore isn't high on the walkers' agenda. Pennine Wayfarers have two routes across it and seem to enjoy neither. This is a wide, almost level moorland cut by Deepdale and Baldersdale. There is army activity in the area, but the routes steer clear of firing ranges. The walks are varied from easy to difficult. The easy walk explores man's attempts to cross Stainmore from darkest prehistoric times to the present day. A boggy walk in search of a "slate" quarry can be attempted. A lengthy walk around Baldersdale is for hard walkers to try in good weather. The Pennine Way main route and an alternative route are combined to form a circular walk from Bowes. Together, the routes demonstrate how immensely varied Stainmore really is.

WALK 15: STAINMORE PASS

I fear you may look on the dual carriageway A66 as a dangerous, high-speed, lorry-laden Euroroute prone to impenetrable fogs, treacherous crosswinds and sudden snowfalls. It is all these things. Some people find it tedious or boring, but the A66 has a long history behind it and there are interesting things to be seen even within sight of the dual carriageway. The shallow gap in the moorland barrier was gouged out in the Ice Age. Although the gap is a lofty 1,400 feet (430 metres), prehistoric traders recognised its value on cross-country expeditions and prehistoric field patterns exist under the nearby blanket bogs.

The Romans exploited this line and used it as an invasion route to Cumbria from their headquarters at York around AD70. A glance at the map immediately reveals their route over Stainmore, their forts at Bowes (Lavatrae) and Brough (Verterae), plus Maiden Castle nearer to the Stainmore Pass and a rash of signal stations and temporary marching camps. Altogether an impressive line of military communications half-way equal to Hadrian's Wall.

No doubt the road was used in the Dark Ages, but it will have deteriorated with the passage of time. These were unsettled times. Erik Bloodaxe, the last Viking King of York, was murdered on the high pass and his death saw an end to plans for an independent Viking kingdom in the region. The Rey Cross was planted where he died. The stone also marked the boundary between the kingdoms of Northumbria and Strathclyde (England and Scotland if you prefer) until 1042. The Normans used Stainmore as a hunting forest and paused to record the "Rair Croiz de Staynemore" in 1280.

With help from the monasteries a hospice system was established along the road as early as 1171. These places are recalled by placenames such as Old Spital, Spital Park and Spital Grange. Food and shelter were on offer to weary travellers and the provision of local guides suggests that the route was in a poor condition. After drovers and pack-horses had trudged over the pass in their eras, a turnpike was constructed in 1743. Both Bowes and Brough became important coaching centres and the architecture of both villages still speaks of those days. The South Durham and Lancashire Union Railway opened on a parallel route in 1861, but only lasted a century while Durham coke was required for the blast furnaces of the North West.

Coaching inns have been superseded by hotels and transport cafes - all worth a visit. The A66 has become a dual carriageway and an affront to the senses in this wilderness, but a logical development

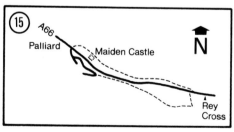

in the light of past history. The walk delves ever so shallowly into that history, concentrating on the visible remnants of former transport routes over the Stainmore Pass. A Roman road, a turnpike, a railway trackbed and pre-dual carriageway tarmac roads are all linked within sight or earshot of the main road. With a bit of discipline the walker can imagine the conditions pertinent to each era, but don't become too glassy-eyed when crossing and re-crossing the dual carriageway as the traffic stops for no-one.

THE ROUTE

Distance:	An easy five mile walk on good tracks and roads.
Maps:	1:50,000 Landranger Sheets 91 or 92
	1:25,000 Pathfinder Sheet 598
Start/Finish:	Stainmore Pass
Getting There:	Drive from Bowes towards Brough and look out for the Cumbria sign on the highest part of the A66.
Parking:	At a lay-by just inside Cumbria.

The parking arrangements for this walk favour motorists travelling from Bowes to Brough. Simply pull into the large lay-by after passing the Cumbria country boundary sign on the highest part of the road. Motorists approaching from the other direction perform U-turns at their peril!

From the lay-by, walk across the county boundary to enter Durham. Look out for the sad stump of stone known as the Rey Cross. This would be entirely anonymous were it not accompanied by an explanatory plaque. Next, and with great care, cross the road and head back into Cumbria. Turn right, off the road, to go through a gate. Turn left to go through another gate and follow a gravel track running parallel to the main road. This climbs slightly and ends at an isolated curve of tarmac. This is a section of the main road immediately pre-dating the dual carriageway. It stands marooned with its fading white lines, a redundant lay-by and a litter bin which was never emptied before the road was severed from the transport network.

There are two gates ahead. Go through the one on the right. An excellent unfenced green road climbs gently uphill. This is the line of the old Roman road which was subsequently improved as a

Brough Castle at the foot of Stainmore Pass

turnpike road. It cuts a wide swathe across the hillside and is in a good state of repair. Keep climbing to pass an old piece of agricultural ironwork (Bamfords Patent Lion Horse Rake) and forge straight through a wet, rushy area which obscures the line of the old road. After passing through a gate, look out for the concentric rubble ramparts of Maiden Castle on the left. This intermediate fortlet stood between the major forts at Bowes and Brough. The surrounding moorlands bear signal stations - the highest being known as Roper Castle. Beyond Maiden Castle the old road runs straight down to the A66 near Palliard Farm. Half of the walk has been completed.

Wait for a chance, then hurry across the busy road and follow a minor road running roughly parallel. This was actually the main road prior to the construction of the dual carriageway, but it carries very little traffic today. At a sharp bend in the road, continue along a fenced gravel track alongside the A66. Note an old pill box on the moor above, strategically sited to defend the road during the War years. There is a point on the track where there are gates to right and left. Go through the gate on the right to walk along the trackbed of the South Durham and Lancashire Union Railway. This curves away from the main road and runs through a rocky cutting to reach an old navvy hut. At this point, turn left through a gap in a wall, cross a small beck and follow a wall straight up to the A66 and the large lay-by.

WALK 16: NORTH STAINMORE AND SLATE QUARRY MOSS

Normally we use maps to answer such questions as "Where are we?" or "Where are we going?" Occasionally the map itself prompts a question which can only be answered by packing the rucksack, pulling on a pair of boots and getting out to do some elementary research. This walk started that way. I noticed a bridleway which wandered over the moors from North Stainmore, only to end abruptly without really getting anywhere. The particular patch of moorland it reached was called Slate Quarry Moss. I wondered if there really was a quarry there, and if there was, could it really be a slate quarry? I knew that Stainmore was entirely composed of sedimentary rocks, so the idea of slate being present was a puzzle. There was only one way to find out for sure.

To cut a long walk short, there was a quarry in that God-forsaken spot and it wasn't strictly a slate quarry. It was a flagstone quarry. Flagstone is a type of sandstone which contains layers of mica flakes which allow it to be split into thin sheets. The end result is rather thicker and less durable than a true slate, but given good supporting timbers a flagstone roof is as good as a slate roof. The bottom line, as always, is economics - if it's on your doorstep it doesn't really matter if it's second rate. There are several buildings on Stainmore with flagstone roofs - on some derelict buildings they are sagging dangerously. True slate is found on later buildings, while the most recent might well feature artificial tiles.

The walk answered my original question, but having seen the approach to Slate Quarry Moss a fresh set of questions arose. The quarry is set in a peaty moorland and dressed flagstones were carted down the moor to North Stainmore. There is plenty of evidence to demonstrate that the carters would use a route until it became impassable, then they would side-step it and gouge out a fresh route. There are numerous boggy grooves around hillsides which display this process well. Perhaps more than a century has passed since the last cart-load of flagstones was brought down from the quarry, no doubt struggling along a deep, muddy trench. The trench is now filled with sphagnum moss, which is nowhere near as firm as the surrounding peat moorland.

How long does it take a peat moorland to regenerate? A century, two centuries, never? One of the suggestions for combating erosion

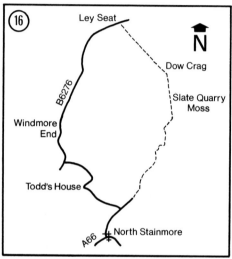

on the hills today is simply to keep people out until the necessary regeneration has taken place. In some areas this just wouldn't occur - the peat moorlands being the most fragile, easily damaged and least likely to repair themselves. Repair schemes initiated elsewhere in the country have proved labour-intensive, yet rely heavily upon volunteers. Sometimes the results have been described as environmentally insensitive. Too often the authorities wait until "disaster area" conditions prevail before they are spurred into action. How much easier the task would be if preventative action was taken the moment problems became apparent. How much different would the approach to Slate Quarry Moss be today if the wasted stone dressings had been tipped on the moorland to provide a firm base for heavy carts? In many parts of the North Pennines routes used for heavy traffic have been provided with a firm base. On Slate Quarry Moss the delicate peat was simply destroyed. The same could be said for heavily walked routes - give them a surface equal to the pounding of booted feet, rather than let areas be trodden to death. Enough said - there's a walk to be done in a little visited part of Stainmore.

THE ROUTE

Distance:	A difficult nine mile moorland walk with an easy ending.
Maps:	1:50,000 Landranger Sheets 91 or 92 1:25,000 Pathfinder Sheet 598
Start/Finish:	North Stainmore
Getting There:	North Stainmore is on the A66 between Brough and the Stainmore Pass. Be careful - it is easily missed.
Parking:	Limited. Ask for permission at the Punch Bowl Hotel.

North Stainmore lies on an awkward bend on the A66. Look out for it carefully, then get off the road quickly and safely. Try asking for permission to park at the Punch Bowl Hotel, in return for patronage. Follow a minor road uphill through the bleak little settlement of North Stainmore. After ³/₄ mile the road ends at two gates. Go through the gate on the right, then turn left immediately and walk uphill to go through another gate. Follow an obvious gravel track alongside waterfalls for another ³/₄ mile to emerge on open moorlands. A number of boggy grooves curve around a spur of moorland ahead, converging to cross a beck. The crossing is quite neat - exploiting a flat slab of rock above a small waterfall. After curving around another moorland spur the track makes a messy crossing of another beck. The track heads northwards and less distinctly uphill on a wet moorland slope. After going through a gate a short ascent on firm ground is followed by a plunge into a pus-green bog.

The line of the track is obvious - a bright green streak across a dun moorland. Unfortunately the sphagnum moss conceals a channel of indeterminate depth and it cannot be followed in safety. The best course to take is to walk on the left side of this mess, but even then there are awkward side-channels which need to be negotiated.

Circuitous detours make this ¼ mile section seem endless. Boots and wellies could be lost in this morass. Wet feet are almost certainly guaranteed. After crossing a small beck the ground suddenly becomes quite firm.

Ahead are a series of low, stony mounds - the so-called slate quarry. The track finally ends here. Spend time browsing around this one-time hive of activity. Build a cairn as a monument to your visit. Build a shelter if the weather is foul. The flat stones are ideal for rough drystone constructions. These are just delaying tactics offered to take your mind off a return journey through that awful bog.

Bail out as follows to avoid such a return: Walk away from the quarry on a northwards line for ½ mile to the shoulder of moorland called Dow Crag around 1,800 feet (550 metres). Turn left to walk north-west along a fence aligned to the Durham and Cumbria county boundary. Notice the odd boundary stone inscribed with numbers in ascending order. These aren't strictly continuous as some specimens have sunk into the soft peat. After a mile of following the boundary the B6276 is reached at Ley Seat. Turn left to walk down the road into Cumbria for 2½ miles. A minor road on the left returns to North Stainmore within two miles. The road passes through pleasant limestone country which contrasts starkly with the stern moors above. Aim for the Punch Bowl Hotel - you could probably do with a drink.

WALK 17: BALDERSDALE AND COTHERSTONE MOOR

This walk explores Baldersdale and its surrounding moorlands and provides a long, hard day's walk. Good navigation is required and the route would seem an endless treadmill in wet weather or poor visibility. Basically, the River Balder is traced almost to its source above Balderhead Reservoir. Wide, rolling moors are a feature of the route, with route-finding aided by the presence of prominent boundary fences. A short section of the Pennine Way completes the circuit.

The mid-point of the Pennine Way occurs at Baldersdale. Wayfarers digest this with muted celebration. The next few miles both one way and the other are uninspiring. Sober thoughts occupy their minds as the nearest pub is several miles away. The huge Balderhead Reservoir dam frowns on their efforts so far. Some of the Pennine Wayfarers stay at the Youth Hostel at the foot of the dam. They are grateful for the provision of accommodation in this area, but don't feel drawn to explore the surroundings.

Most of the dale is given over to reservoirs - Balderhead Reservoir, Blackton Reservoir and Hury Reservoir. Some publicity was afforded to the area through the lifestyle of Hannah Hauxwell. Hannah used to live close to the Youth Hostel at Birk Hatt Farm and has been the subject of television documentaries and books. She has been persuaded to settle further down-dale, but her story will ever provide an insight onto the life and work of the dale. Shepherds seem to have had a hard life in this area. The walk passes a number of small sheepfolds equipped with small, stone shelters. In these endless acres, shepherding on foot in all weathers remains a solitary occupation for hardy dalesfolk.

The name of Baldersdale has a good Norse ring about it. Walker Scott's "Rokeby" attributes this to Danish invaders. He wrote that they:

> Fixed on each vale a Runic name,
> Reared high their altar's rugged stone,
> And gave their Gods the land they won.
> Then, Balder, one bleak garth was thine,
> And one sweet brooklet's silver line.

Stirring stuff, but a pity the river has been swallowed almost in its entirety by the reservoirs. The last remaining stretch of freely flowing water is traced in the early part of the walk.

THE ROUTE

Distance:	A difficult 13 mile moorland walk with few paths.
Maps:	1:50,000 Landranger Sheets 91 or 92
	1:25,000 Pathfinder Sheet 598
Start/Finish:	Balder Head
Getting There:	Balder Head is at the end of a minor road serving Baldersdale. Leave the B6277 at Romaldkirk.
Parking:	At the very end of the minor road at Balder Head.

The tarmac road running the length of Baldersdale ends at Balder

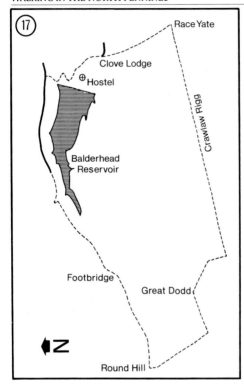

Head with a parking space. A wide gravel track continues further. Follow this track until it has described a tight loop around a narrow ravine. A gate on the right gives access to open moorlands. A rushy ditch climbing gently uphill marks the way ahead. A small sheepfold and ruined hut are passed. After walking another ³/₄ mile a similar fold and hut are passed. Go through a gateway in a ruined wall and walk downhill to the confluence of Black Beck and Balder Beck.

Cross Black Beck by using a footbridge, but don't cross Balder Beck yet - despite the presence of a footbridge. Instead, climb up the moorland spur between the two becks and keep to the high ground overlooking Balder Beck. Proceed upstream in this manner, noting yet another fold and hut close to the bank of Balder Beck. A black hut on wheels is passed (if it hasn't been rolled away to another place) and this is the only shelter for miles around. The path being followed is rather vague - no more than a sheep trod despite the map insisting on the presence of a bridleway. The path drifts down to run alongside the beck. Cross the beck at any point and continue walking upstream to reach a fence which is aligned to the Cumbria and Durham county boundary.

Turn left to follow the fence over the spur of moorland called Round Hill. The angles described by the fence are a useful guide and the county boundary runs in a series of straight lines as follows: one mile roughly south-south-east; $^{3}/_{4}$ mile roughly east-north-east; $^{1}/_{2}$ mile roughly south-east; and $^{1}/_{4}$ mile roughly southwards. There are also a few boundary stones along this line which are inscribed with numbers in descending order.

Look out for a prominent fence-line which shoots off east-north-east for $3^{1}/_{2}$ miles along Crawlaw Rigg. The walker appears to be marooned on an immense, flat plain, which is bad enough, but conditions underfoot are worse. Throughout this moorland trek the ground is boggy, heathery, pitted with holes, and sometimes features tussocky grass or even stones. This can be extremely testing country in bad weather. The trudge along Crawlaw Rigg seems endless. Note the curious flat-topped hill called Shackleborough. This acts as a sort of central pivot to the circuit. Only when you have to look back over your left shoulder to find it can you be sure that the trek along Crawlaw Rigg is coming to an end.

It happens suddenly at Race Yate. The Pennine Way crosses at right angles at the corner of a wall. Simply turn left to abandon the fence and walk downhill for a mile over grassy moorland. The farm of Clove Lodge is reached, which sometimes offers teas and snacks to tired walkers. The Pennine Way continues down to a bridge over a narrow part of Blackton Reservoir. Turn left once across the bridge and follow a zig-zag road up to a minor road. Turn left on the minor road and walk $1^{1}/_{4}$ miles to return to the parking space at the end of the road. The start/finish of this walk can be adapted to suit walkers staying at the Youth Hostel, which is only slightly off-route.

WALK 18: BOWES AND THE PENNINE WAY

It is usual to think of the Pennine Way as a purely linear route, but in places there are alternative routes which deviate from the main route and join up again later. The Pennine Way main route makes a bee-line across the Stainmore wastes to reach the Youth Hostel in Baldersdale. A softer option is available which takes Wayfarers

Goldsborough's gritstone cap is a notable landmark

down to Bowes on the way to Baldersdale. The walk offered here makes use of the "main route" and "Bowes loop" to create a circular walk out of the Pennine Way.

This is fairly straight forward moorland walking, but it is best reserved for periods of fine weather. The paths and tracks used by the Pennine Way are fairly well trodden, but in one or two places rather vague. There is a track rising onto the moors from Battle Hill which can be used to shorten the route, cutting about 1½ miles off the total. Unfortunately, the short-cut misses out the chance of teas and snacks at Clove Lodge in Baldersdale. After walking the two sections of the Pennine Way, it will be noticed from a study of the paths that more people seem to stick to the main route.

Whatever spare time is available can be used to make a thorough exploration of Bowes. Now that the traffic has been diverted around the village it has become a pleasant place. The Romans built their fort of Lavatrae there and the basic grassy ramparts can still be traced. The masonry was incorporated into Bowes Castle - a solid watch-tower constructed in 1170 to keep an eye on the Stainmore approaches. This was an unsettled borderland area where the free

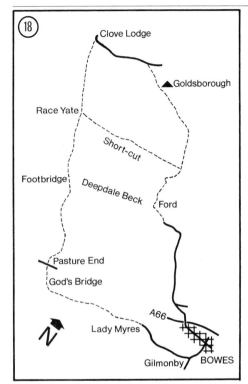

flow of traffic was frequently hampered in times of strife. With the coming of a good turnpike road the village became an important coaching centre - the next one over the pass being Brough. The Ancient Unicorn is a good "horsey" name for a coaching inn and is well worth a visit. Other buildings have coaching connections. The church of St. Giles is an interesting structure worth exploring. There is also a ruinous railway station.

Charles Dickens visited Bowes and Teesdale in 1838. He was collecting information about the notorious "Yorkshire Schools" where a schoolboy could expect to lead a life of abject misery, suffering from poor health, frequent beatings and emerging poorly educated at the end of it. Boarders were often sent out to work on surrounding farms, earning money for their cruel headmasters. Dotheboys Hall, at one end of Bowes, was such a place. At least one pupil of the school lies buried in the churchyard of St. Giles. Some of Dickens' information was gleaned at the bar of the Ancient Unicorn, but he also met William Shaw, who was the headmaster of "Shaw's Academy" as Dotheboys Hall was known. William Shaw was transformed into "Wackford

Squeers" by Dickens' pen and the subsequent outcry against the "Yorkshire Schools" resulted in their ultimate closure. William Shaw also lies buried in the churchyard. Part of Dotheboys Hall was demolished and the remainder stands as a series of private dwellings. Special "Dickens Tours" are operated from Barnard Castle and feature a guide in period costume. It's all harmless fun. If you're keen you could research a number of places with Dickens connections and link them together in a long distance walk.

THE ROUTE

Distance:	A moderate 12 mile moorland walk on good paths.
Maps:	1:50,000 Landranger Sheet 92
	1:25,000 Pathfinder Sheet 598
Start/Finish:	Bowes
Getting There:	Bowes lies off the A66 between Scotch Corner and Brough. Also reached via the A67 from Barnard Castle.
Parking:	Near the crossroads in Bowes.

From the village crossroads walk past the Ancient Unicorn, St. Giles' church and Dotheboys Hall. Cross the road bridge over the busy A66 and continue uphill to a junction. Turn left and follow a minor road for nearly 1½ miles to West Stoney Keld Farm. Surely the MOD "Poison Gas" signs are no longer required along this road, but they continue to be renewed. An obvious track leads down to the atmospheric thatched ruin of Levy Pool. Deepdale Beck must be forded at this point - which could mean wet feet.

The Pennine Way is a little indistinct for the next ½ mile. It climbs the hillside, descends to a minor beck, then climbs up to join a fence by a ruined wall. The fence and wall are followed onwards across the moors and the route is rather like a roller-coaster ride for ½ mile. Branch left across open moorland away from the perimeter of an army firing range. Aim for Goldsborough - the prominent hump of moorland capped with a huge disc of gritstone. If time allows, explore the tumbled blocks, inspect the overhanging cliffs and climb to the 1,274 feet (388 metres) summit. The Pennine Way merely crosses the shoulder of the hill and gradually descends to a road.

Turn left to follow the road for a mile to Clove Lodge. Teas and snacks are sometimes on offer at the farmhouse. Just before the farm, a Pennine Way signpost points up a long, moorland slope on the left. Over a mile of open, grassy moorland is ascended on a fairly good path to reach 1,400 feet (420 metres) on Race Yate. The view all round takes in the broad Stainmore wastes, with Mickle Fell to the north-west and Rogan's Seat directly southwards. Eastwards are green pastures and the distant flares of the Teesmouth refineries. A wall leads straight down from Race Yate into Deepdale. A footbridge crosses Deepdale Beck and on the ascent heather becomes dominant. A tumbled ruin of stones - no more than a simple hut in times gone by - rejoices in the name of Ravock Castle. The path eventually reaches Pasture End.

Just as the walker becomes attuned to the peace and desolation of the moors, the A66 comes as a violent interruption. Hurry straight across and continue downhill on a good track. The track goes under the disused South Durham and Lancashire Union Railway and reaches God's Bridge. Study God's Bridge from beneath to appreciate that this is an entirely natural feature. It takes a lot of rain to make the River Greta flow through this limestone dale, but when it runs the water goes under this massive limestone slab. Normally, the river bed is dry except for a dark pool lurking beneath God's Bridge.

Bear left once across God's Bridge, going though a gate and up a field to reach West Mellwaters Farm. Bowes is three miles away, reached by linking a series of farms. A track leads from West to East Mellwaters. Pennine Way signposts show the way to a footbridge across Sleightholme Beck to reach West Charity Farm. A track runs to Lady Mires Farm and a road continues to Gilmonby. Turn left at Gilmonby to return to Bowes. On entering the village, Back Lane can be used to reach Bowes Castle and St. Giles' church, otherwise continue straight onwards for the crossroads and the Ancient Unicorn.

Lower Tees Section

WALK 19: Barnard Castle and the Tees
WALK 20: Cotherstone and Romaldkirk
WALK 21: Hamsterley Forest

All three of these walks are outside of the designated AONB, but they offer easy walking in places often visited on tours of the North Pennines. Barnard Castle is a natural gateway to Teesdale and the place has great character. Interesting riverside footpaths are available from the town. Cotherstone and Romaldkirk are scenic villages set around pleasant greens. They are linked in a circuit which involves following part of the River Tees. Hamsterley Forest is the odd one out - consigned to this section for want of somewhere to put it. It is neither part of Teesdale nor Weardale. It is the only walk in the whole guide which is exclusively confined to a forest plantation. It is remarkably interesting and an eye-opener for those who consider forest trails to be monotonous.

WALK 19: BARNARD CASTLE AND THE TEES

Barnard Castle is very peripheral to the North Pennines, but it is a town of great character and interest and a natural gateway to the delights of Teesdale. Many visitors to the North Pennines are drawn time and time again to this ancient market town, perhaps because of its castle or the splendid Bowes Museum. Anyone stopping here might as well walk here too. There are a series of easy waymarked routes which wander upstream along the River Tees. Two of these routes are offered in a combined form, as they are both rather short in themselves. One uses a series of woodland paths laid out a century ago by George Edwards. The route passes through mixed woodlands of slow growing oak, quick growing sycamore, sturdy pines and beeches, ash and yews. In season there are bluebells, ramsons, heather and bilberry - all depending on light, shade and soil. The other waymarked path links a series of farm access tracks and paths. Towler Hill Farm is visited, where Turner planted his easel and painted a view of the Tees and Barnard Castle in 1816. Both walks are described as a single route, though they could be done separately. Extensions could be made to reach Cotherstone, if required. Whatever option is chosen, Barnard Castle merits a thorough exploration.

The Castle, from which Barnard Castle takes its name, was built in the twelfth century by Bernard Baliol. Its extensive curtain wall encloses a park-like interior. The bridge which spans the River Tees below is thought to date from 1569, but replaces other structures and fords dating back to Roman times. The town lies on the course of a Roman road. The Market Cross isn't a cross at all, but a substantial octagonal building gifted to the town by Thomas Breaks in 1747. It has been variously pressed into service as a town hall, courthouse and jail, as well as sundry other civic uses. The street market wouldn't look the same without it. Visitors as varied as Cromwell and Dickens have passed through Barnard Castle. Railways came in the 1850s. The River Tees was spanned by a mighty viaduct in 1861, but this was demolished a century later, leaving only the immense supporting buttresses.

The Bowes Museum appears totally out of character with the town, but no-one ever complains at the sight of this huge, grand, French-style edifice set in beautifully complimentary gardens. The museum started as a project in 1860 under the patronage of John and Josephine Bowes. John was the son of the 10th Earl of Strathmore and had bags of money behind him. Josephine was a Parisian actress and artist with a keen sense of taste. Together they amassed a vast collection of European arts in a mere fifteen years. There is just too much to take in during a single visit, so visitors keep coming back again and again to study a bit more each time.

There's plenty more to see in Barnard Castle, including old churches and quaint shops. Each visit to the town can be used to take in another short walk - perhaps downstream on the Tees next time to have a look at Egglestone Abbey, or staying close to town to have a better look at the ravine of Percy Beck. After exploring the area a few times you'll find it second nature to call the town by its nickname - "Barney".

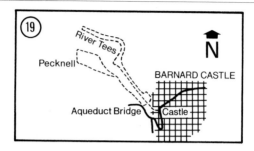

THE ROUTE

Distance: An easy eight mile low-level walk on good tracks and paths.

Maps: 1:50,000 Landranger Sheet 92
1:25,000 Outdoor Leisure Sheet 31

Start/Finish: Barnard Castle

Getting There: Barnard Castle is easily reached by main roads from Bishop Auckland, Darlington, Scotch Corner and Bowes.

Parking: At the car park close to the Tourist Information Centre.

Starting from the car park near the Tourist Information Centre, walk down the wide, attractive Galgate to reach the little park at Scar Top. There is an information board at this point which gives brief notes about three waymarked walks which radiate into the surrounding countryside. Our walk combines the two which explore the River Tees upstream from Barnard Castle. The Castle, incidentally, is immediately available for a quick visit at the start.

Walk downhill past the Castle entrance and turn right to start following the River Tees upstream. Walk past an aqueduct bridge without crossing it, then cross a nearby footbridge over Percy Beck. The route wanders through varied and interesting woodlands for nearly 1³/₄ miles, keeping always to the most obvious riverside paths. On the way, woodland scents vary from rank ramsons and fungi to sweet honeysuckle in season. All that remains of the lofty Tees Viaduct can be seen later - two supporting stone buttresses;

one on each side of the river. The riverside path is known as the "Rock Walk" and includes features such as the "Wishing Stones" (you get a free wish when you walk between them) and a stone staircase built into a cliff to cope with an awkward bit of river bank.

The path eventually reaches a gate and proceeds into a meadow away from the river. A short distance into the meadow, turn right to go through a gate and follow a path steeply uphill. This short ascent leads out onto level fields and the view demonstrates how deeply entrenched the River Tees is in this part of the country. Turn right to follow the field boundaries close to the woodland edge for a mile. This leads to an old railway trackbed. It is possible to walk out to the end of the old viaduct buttress and peep over the parapet to the twin buttress across the Tees. To continue the walk, use either a footpath at the edge of the woodland, or one just inside it, to return to Barnard Castle. Both paths ultimately descend to Percy Beck after ½ mile. Barnard Castle is close at hand for anyone wanting to end the walk early.

To link with another waymarked walk, follow Percy Beck down to the River Tees, turn left, then right to cross the aqueduct bridge. Turn right again to pick up a track running upstream alongside the Tees. In ½ mile this leads to a house where a waymark reveals a path into a wood. The path climbs up to the other buttress of the Tees Viaduct and crosses the old trackbed just behind it. Waymarks indicate the route across fields to join the access track running to Towler Hill Farm. Follow this track almost to the farm, then turn left to follow another track across fields. Turn left again to go under an old railway bridge. Yet another left turn reveals a waymarked path across fields which eventually joins another track. Turn right this time and follow the track back towards Barnard Castle. It turns out to be the track used from the aqueduct bridge. This time, however, don't cross the aqueduct bridge, but cross the fine old stone bridge to re-enter town by the main road. This leads through the Market Place and there are plenty of fine buildings and shops to admire along the way.

WALK 20: COTHERSTONE AND ROMALDKIRK

This walk starts from Cotherstone, toys with the Tees for a bit, then heads for Romaldkirk. After descending to the Tees at Eggleston Bridge the route climbs up flights of steps engineered by local ramblers to reach higher pastures. A lofty viewpoint at Percy Mere is visited before the route finally runs down to the Tees, crosses it and climbs back up to Cotherstone. This is an easy walk, but route-finding can be a bit fiddly in places. There are a number of waymarks, but an eye needs to be kept peeled for them. All the gates and stiles are in place, but careful map-work is necessary.

Also requiring care are a couple of rocky areas. One is a recommended detour from Woden Croft down to the River Tees. The maps maintain that this is a right of way, but to follow it in its entirety would be very difficult and dangerous. Have a look at the Tees by this route, but be sure to climb back up to the fields for safer and easier walking to continue. The viewpoint of Percy Mere could also be dangerous, as the ground suddenly falls away to the River Tees. A notable accident occurred here when the last of the Fitzhughs - Lords of Romaldkirk - fell to his death. He was out hunting when an old lady warned him to go home. As in all romantic tales, he spurned the warning, should have known better than to chase something as unusual as a white deer at nightfall and realised only too late that he was on the brink of Percy Mere. History recorded his death, then moved on.

The Fitzhughs occupied a twelfth century castle on Hallgarth Hill at Cotherstone. The building has gone, leaving only the defensive hill-site. The village hardly bothers to boast about it. In any case, with charms such as Cotherstone's there is no need. Several fine cottages stand around two linear greens and colourful gardens form proud displays. Romaldkirk has a twelfth century church which contains some Saxon stonework. In fact, there have been a number of additions and subtractions to the building which makes it very interesting to study. Perhaps its oddest feature is the tracery of its east window. Somehow, it just doesn't look right and one wonders if the design was ever committed to paper before being cut from stone. There is also a blocked-up north doorway which is supposed to have the Devil on the other side. Romaldkirk is as colourful as Cotherstone, but beats its neighbour by showing off three village greens, plus stocks and an old pump. While the River Tees is only seen from time to time on this walk, the villages make up for lost interest with their generous displays and traditional pubs. Eggleston is the next village up Teesdale, but it lies slightly off-route. Eggleston Bridge is crossed nearby - an impressive double-arched structure with a massive central pier. It was built in the seventeenth century, but is thought to replace a bridge built in the fifteenth century.

Charles Dickens visited Teesdale in 1838. He was collecting information about the notorious "Yorkshire Schools" where a schoolboy could expect to lead a life of abject misery. Woden Croft was such a school, now converted to a farm. Richard Cobden - "Apostle of Free Trade" - was educated there and "could never afterwards endure to speak" of the time he spent there. The buildings and a walled garden show how highly organised the place must have been.

THE ROUTE

Distance:	An easy seven mile low-level walk on paths.
Maps:	1:50,000 Landranger Sheet 92
	1:25,000 Outdoor Leisure Sheet 31
Start/Finish:	Cotherstone
Getting There:	Cotherstone is on the B6277 between Barnard Castle and Middleton-in-Teesdale.
Parking:	Small spaces in the village.
	Ask permission if in doubt.

From the Fox and Hounds pub in Cotherstone, walk straight across the B6277 road to follow a narrow tarmac road steeply downhill. This reaches a small open space by the riverside, where cars might be parked. Hallgarth Hill, site of an old castle, overlooks this area. Turn left to cross the River Balder by a footbridge, but don't cross the longer footbridge over the River Tees - that comes later in the day to return to Cotherstone. Instead, follow the River Tees upstream on a wooded path which gradually moves away from the river. The path follows the woodland edge past an old walled garden to reach Woden Croft - once one of the notorious "Yorkshire Schools". Pass between the buildings on a good track, then stay close to the woods

103

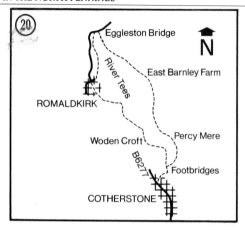

to find a gate on the right. This gives access to a path which runs back down to the River Tees. The river bed is attractively rocky and is worth a visit, but go no further as the ground can be rough and dangerous. The maps maintain that there is a right of way, but it isn't in a fit state to follow. Retrace steps to the fields above, turn right and continue to an old farmhouse at Low Garth. Follow the access track only a short way from the building, then branch right up the field to go through a tiny gate. Cross two fields to reach an avenue of trees. Turn right to locate a track running straight through the avenue, reaching Romaldkirk 2³/₄ miles from Cotherstone.

The track reaches a crossroads in Romaldkirk. Turn right and walk down past the green, then left along a walled lane which becomes quite narrow. Cross Beer Beck by a small footbridge, then climb a wall stile on the left. Cross three fields - the first two diagonally and the last one by following the edge of the riverside wood. On reaching the B6281 road ³/₄ mile from Romaldkirk, turn right to cross Eggleston Bridge, pausing to admire its splendid form. Eggleston Hall and village are a short way uphill, but off-route.

After crossing Eggleston Bridge, turn right to follow the River Tees downstream. A narrow tarmac road starts the journey, passing a small sports field changing room. Later, a stile on the left leads to a series of steps uphill through flowery woodlands. On leaving the
104

woods, move away from the woodland edge slightly to cross a field, then cross the next field diagonally and continue to East Barnley Farm. Don't use the access tracks on the left, but walk past all the buildings, bear right and walk across a field to reach Raygill Beck. Cross the steep-sided beck, aim for a solitary oak tree and continue roughly in the same direction to reach the boundary of Shipley Wood. Later, the path moves away from the woodland edge, but first make a slight detour into the wood to stand on top of Percymere Rock. This overlooks the Tees, the deep, wooded dale, and gives far-reaching views over Stainmore to the lopped-off summits of Goldsborough and Shacklesborough.

The path which branches away from the woodland edge later rejoins it, then follow the boundary downhill. Go through a caravan site, making an exit by the toilets to continue down to the River Tees. Cross the river by the long footbridge, turn left to cross the footbridge over the River Balder, then turn right to walk back up the narrow tarmac road to Cotherstone.

WALK 21: HAMSTERLEY FOREST

Hamsterley Forest is the largest forest in the North Pennines and the walk offered is the only one in this guide which is exclusively confined to a forestry plantation. There are six colour-coded waymarked trails in the forest and the particular one chosen for this guide is the High Acton Walk. This is the longest trail and it goes higher than the rest, but the walk itself is quite easy and sticks to good tracks and paths. In fact, there is a part of the route where either a wide track or a narrow path can be used. The waymarks prevent walkers from getting lost as there is a network of tracks in this, the largest and quietest part of the forest. A map should still be carried, if only for reference. Also, there is a leaflet which details the range of trails and offers useful information about planting phases. With one of these leaflets, you will know that a tree bearing a mark JL P31 means that it is a Japanese Larch which was planted in 1931. The route could be adapted to take in other waymarked trails, or any other path or track. Some of the tracks leave the forest completely and allow access to the surrounding moors.

A visitor centre has been established at the Bedburn end of the forest and this gives a useful introduction to the life and work of the forest. Motorists pay a toll to cover driving along the forest road and parking at one of the car parks or picnic sites. A mountain bike hire allows non-walkers to tear around the forest tracks, though very few riders reach the High Acton Walk. Forest rangers occasionally conduct special-interest tours for those with enquiring minds and a thirst for knowledge. This is the only real forest in the book - so make the most of it.

The Grove, at the centre of Hamsterley Forest, was once the centre of a farming and sporting estate. There were plantations and patches of woodland. When the Forestry Commission bought the estate in 1927 they were quick to blanket the whole area with fast-growing conifers. At that time the idea was to build up reserves of growing trees as quickly as possible. Attitudes within the Commission have changed over the years. There are few plantations in the North Pennines and Hamsterley Forest is the largest and oldest. Some parts now display mature stands, but the forest has been managed long enough to feature a mixture of ages and species of trees. Sitka spruce is dominant, but there is Scots pine too. Lodgepole pine and Norway spruce are important, along with larches. There are patches of broadleaved woods, such as Pennington Plantaion, and plenty of beckside growths. The number of tree species is around sixty and this allows a varied wildlife to flourish.

There are shy roe deer, badgers and squirrels to be noted by patient observers. Woodcocks and woodpeckers can be seen and

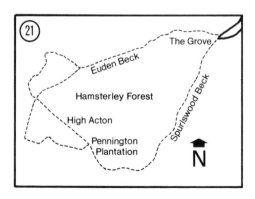

heard. Herons and dippers feed in the watercourses. Finches and crossbills find food. Hen harriers and sparrowhawks represent birds of prey. Owls and bats are present. Insects include dragonflies, moths and butterflies. Flora varies from orchids in the unplanted beckside wetlands to delicate ferns on King's Crag. Fungi rise up from the unlit forest floor. The variety of species is a testimony to the type of forest management currently practised at Hamsterley Forest. Conservation and crop rotation can go hand in hand. This isn't a monoblock plantation, but a place to walk and enjoy a great variety of interesting scenes.

THE ROUTE

Distance:	An easy eight mile forest walk on good tracks and paths.
Maps:	1:50,000 Landranger Sheet 92
	1:25,000 Outdoor Leisure Sheet 31
Start/Finish:	The Grove, Hamsterley Forest.
Getting There:	The Grove is in the forest and is best approached from the villages of Hamsterley or Woodland.
Parking:	At The Grove car park.

After parking at The Grove car park, face the large house and walk to the left of it. Follow only the orange waymarks, which indicate the route of the High Acton Walk. (The only other waymarks near The Grove are the purple ones for the Redford Walk.) The track runs past a group of buildings, then settles down to follow Euden Beck upstream through the forest. Junctions with other tracks are waymarked. Look across the beck to the frowning face of King's Crag. About 2¼ miles out from The Grove there is a choice of routes - using either a footpath or a track. It really depends on the weather. In wet weather it isn't recommended to go squelching along a narrow path under dripping trees. The two alternatives cross later, so it is always possible to switch from one to the other if you feel you made the wrong choice.

The footpath follows Acton Beck, a tributary of Euden Beck, climbing for ¾ mile. It passes the ruins of Neighbour Moor House, which once enjoyed an open prospect before being swallowed by the plantation. The track, on the other hand, twists and turns uphill, covering 1½ miles before crossing Acton Beck. From this point the situation is reversed - the track takes the short route and the footpath does all the twisting and turning. The track runs in a straight line for a mile, peaking at High Acton Currick at 1,280 feet (390 metres) to reach Pennington Plantation. The footpath takes 1¾ miles, climbing to the edge of the forest at 1,410 feet (430 metres). There are views out across Eggleston Common before the track heads for Pennington Plantation.

Pennington Plantation is a beechwood with a special boast to make. It is one of the highest beechwoods in the country at 1,200 feet (360 metres). The trees are not as tall and stately as, say, the Chiltern beeches, but they make a refreshing change from the spruces, pines and firs observed so far along the walk.

The final 3¼ miles of the route use a track which closely follows Spurlswood Beck downstream. There is an attractive mixture of trees alongside the beck, with views out of the forest to the moorlands of Woodland Fell. The orange waymarks continue to show the way, but green waymarks also appear, marking the Spurlswood Beck Trail. Use either route to walk down to Blackling Hole car park. The orange route is easier and more direct, but the green route is only slightly longer and harder. The advantage of the green route is that it has more variety, including an old millstone quarry complete with a millstone, with a descent via the attractive Whisky Gill. Whichever route is chosen, explore the pleasant surroundings of the Blackling Hole car park. Look for the waterfall - Blackling Hole is the dark pool beneath it. The forest drive continuing downstream from Blackling Hole is a rough-surfaced track, but it is used by cars. It leads straight back to The Grove and the end of the walk.

If you liked the walk, why not try some of the other waymarked forest trails another day? Details of each one are contained in a leaflet available from the visitor centre.

Middleton-in-Teesdale is a natural walking centre and it is a neat place which owes its development to the London Lead Company. Lead mining is most evident on a walk around Monks Moor, passing a number of old sites. The Pennine Way passes close to Middleton and offers a route over to Lunedale and Grassholme Reservoir. In the other direction, the Pennine Way enjoys a spell of easy riverside rambling upstream on the River Tees. This provides a charming route through flowery meadows to reach Low Force. The Bowlees Visitor Centre is close to hand at that point and well equipped to help the walker understand something of Teesdale's floral merits. Walks from Middleton traditionally start from the black and yellow painted cast iron drinking fountain planted by the "Quaker Company".

WALK 22: MIDDLETON AND MONKS MOOR

This walk links two dale-head mining sites using a series of paths, tracks and minor roads. A narrow tarmac road runs up Hudeshope from Middleton-in-Teesdale, but this can be avoided by using a permissive path called the King's Walk. The woodland walk is followed by a walk through the devastated dale-head. A moorland track crosses over to the head of Great Eggleshope, where mining is also evident. The return to Middleton is largely by road, but there are fine views over this part of Teesdale and beyond.

The London Lead Company made Middleton-in-Teesdale their headquarters and set about re-ordering and extending the town. Middleton House, rather away from the centre of town, was the superintendent's house. It was built in 1815 and served its purpose

109

until mining ceased in 1905. It is now a high-class grouse-shooting venue and has received royal patronage. When Robert Bainbridge retired from the post of superintendent a collection made by the employees of the "Quaker Company" furnished him with several gifts. The remaining money was used to erect the cast-iron drinking fountain in Middleton and a twin structure at Nenthead. A town trail will reveal the workaday buildings associated with the company, such as a blacksmith's shop, corn mill, school and co-op - all now converted to some other use. New Town was developed as a model housing estate for the workers, or at least for those deemed to be most deserving of the accommodation. Loyalty to the company was well rewarded. A piped water supply was brought into town and in time some 90% of the working population of Middleton were employed by the company.

There is little evidence of lead mining to be seen in the town, but Hudeshope abounds in remains. All is quiet these days, as Nature slowly patches up the holes and heals the scars. Thomas Gibson walked to work here and wrote of noisier days:

> On my left hand Coldberry Mine appears;
> The din of mills and jiggers strike the ears.

Coldberry Mine has left huge scars in the form of levels, hushes, such as the tremendous Coldberry Gutter, and ruined buildings of all kinds. The mills are tumbled and the washing floors are overgrown. This is only Hudeshope - the lead veins continue through the hills to adjacent dale-heads where similar despoilation has occurred. It all makes for an interesting study, but wary walkers will stay on the paths and tracks, well away from hidden holes and tottery sheds.

Lead wasn't the only commodity to be gained in Hudeshope. The Parker family opened a limestone quarry and a series of limekilns to provide abundant supplies of lime. This was used to break up the clay soils and bring areas of acid moorland into cultivation. It also provided mortar for the building schemes initiated in Middleton. The huge kilns are noted early in the walk - the first of them being built in 1840. Also near Middleton, but on the opposite side of the River Tees, are large quarries along the line of the Whin Sill.

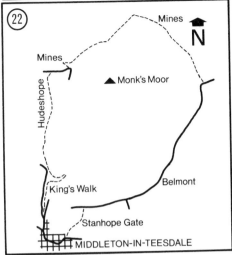

The walk over Monks Moor gives a view over a remote and unfrequented area of high moorlands. This is an area which has been left largely unexplored in this guide, except for noting the route of the Teesdale Watershed Walk. Walkers inspired by the desolate scene may wish to explore it further, but this is a rough and trackless waste with few aids to navigation. The walk described takes the easiest course over the moor and sticks to its lead mining theme.

THE ROUTE

Distance:	An easy ten mile moorland walk on paths, tracks and roads.
Maps:	1:50,000 Landranger Sheet 92
	1:25,000 Outdoor Leisure Sheet 31
Start/Finish:	Middleton-in-Teesdale
Getting There:	Middleton can be reached from Barnard Castle or Alston (B6277), Brough (B6276) or Stanhope (B6278).
Parking:	By the drinking fountain in Middleton.

From the drinking fountain in Middleton, walk through the centre of town and take the Weardale road steeply uphill. There is a narrow tarmac road branching off to the left and only a short way along this there is a waymarked path called the King's Walk on the right. This path runs for over a mile though mixed woodlands. It goes gently uphill, bears right, then left, crosses Snaisgill Beck by a footbridge, then goes left to the woodland edge and gradually down to a good track. There are a series of large limekilns nearby which should be inspected. Walk past these to discover a limestone quarry which fed the kilns. Keep high beyond the quarry to locate a stile over a wall where the path leaves the woods.

The path continues by following the edge of the woodland further up Hudeshope. A gradual descent allows the path to run close to Hudeshope Beck, following it upstream. The hillside on the right is crinkly with old hushes which were once scoured out by releasing dammed water. Old ruins and spoil heaps are populated by scores of rabbits. The path becomes wider and clearer for a while, then crosses Marl Beck. Go over a stile at this point, then turn right to walk uphill to join a minor road about three miles from Middleton. Look around the devastated dale-head, noting the enormous scar of Coldberry Gutter, caused by repeated hushing. The ruins of Coldberry Mine are quite evident, featuring levels, spoil heaps, old buildings and overgrown washing floors.

Turn right to follow the minor road ¼ mile to a sharp bend. Immediately before the sharp bend, on the left, is a substantial mining track. Follow this uphill, swing sharply right, then left. On the right is another track which leads from Hudeshope over to Great Eggleshope. This track crosses moorlands as high as 1,770 feet (540 metres) and is perfectly obvious on the ground. There are small mines along the way and a small pool on the moor is sometimes occupied by a raucous colony of black-headed gulls. The descent to Great Eggleshope is less clear. Keep to the left of a small beck to avoid difficult ground. Turn right at the bottom, about 1½ miles from the last minor road, to pick up a good track accompanying Great Eggleshope Beck downstream. A cluster of mine buildings are passed and a minor road is reached just over a mile beyond.

Turn right to follow the minor road uphill, looking back at the splendidly sited Middle End Farm. Walk along the road for 2¾ miles, passing Belmont and Stotley Grange. There is a wide-ranging view from this high road, taking in Teesdale, Stainmore and the vast bulk of Mickle Fell, with peeps at other heights around Upper Teesdale. A point is reached where there are footpath signs on both sides of the road. Turn left to follow a wall downhill from the road at this point. Keep to the right of the farm at Stanhope Gate, then follow the course of a very minor beck downhill. All the gates and stiles will be revealed on the way to the road below. Simply turn right on the road to walk into Middleton, perhaps embarking on a town trail to identify buildings from the "Quaker Company" years.

WALK 23: MIDDLETON AND GRASSHOLME

This is an easy circuit which has more miles of paths available than the map cares to admit. The Pennine Way is traced from Middleton-in-Teesdale over to Grassholme in Lunedale. This part of the walk is potentially confusing, but provided a careful watch is maintained for gates and stiles there should be no problem. This is the Pennine Way, after all! A simple shore walk along the side of Grassholme Reservoir is followed by an untrodden path through a series of fields. A short walk along the disused Tees Valley Railway follows. The old line has been revitalised as the Tees Valley Way. The River Tees is briefly traced on the way back to Middleton.

Throughout this walk, and from several other points in the area, the dark plantation on Kirkcarrion features as a landmark. It looks as if it has a story to tell - and indeed it has. The high ridge was chosen as the site of a tomb for a Brigantean prince called Caryn. Kirkcarrion is therefore Caryn's Church. An excavation in 1804 delved into the tumulus and brought out an urn of charred bones - presumably the same Caryn. The subsequent plantation of Scots pines in this desolate spot have made it into a landmark and also imparted a mysterious air to the place. Few would want to spend the night in that lonely copse, listening to the low moan of the wind, especially as Caryn is believed to wander nocturnally around his desecrated tomb.

Lunedale has been flooded by the narrow Grassholme Reservoir and the larger expanse of Selset Reservoir. Northumbrian Water actively encourages public use of the reservoirs, but the maps don't always detail the range of facilities on offer. Anglers can park and make sport here, while walkers have access to the whole shoreline. Grassholme Reservoir is really quite attractive when the water level is high, but there are curious features to note when the water is low.

The Tees Valley Way crosses an old railway viaduct

Grassholme Bridge was built by the reservoir engineers to maintain a road across the dale. The old bridge was consigned to the depths largely intact. This once-beautiful double-arched bridge occasionally stands high and dry with its beauty marred by flaking mud. Instead of being surrounded by green pastures it stands in a dreary expanse of mudflats. Nearby are several umbrellas, which presumably belonged to anglers before being blown into the reservoir. These stand spiked in the mud like an obscure artistic statement. If there isn't time to complete the whole of this walk, then at least consider the circuit of the reservoir.

As an introduction to Lunedale this walk displays most of what is on offer to walkers. Selset Reservoir has some shore paths too. The upper reaches of the dale take in the slopes of Mickle Fell, where walking opportunities are limited. The Pennine Way takes the shortest course from Lunedale over the ridge to Teesdale. There is another footpath and a bridleway, but these are longer and can't really be tied with other routes to form a practical circuit. Save them for longer through trips, or for times when transport can be arranged to and from the terminal points.

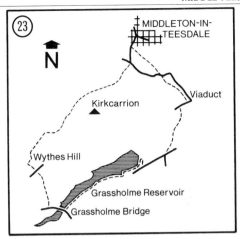

THE ROUTE

Distance: An easy nine mile walk on paths, tracks and roads.
Maps: 1:50,000 Landranger Sheet 91 or 92
1:25,000 Outdoor Leisure Sheet 31
Start/Finish: Middleton-in-Teesdale
Getting There: Middleton can be reached from Barnard Castle or Alston (B6277), Brough (B6276) or Stanhope (B6278).
Parking: By the drinking fountain in Middleton.

From the drinking fountain in Middleton, take the road signposted Brough. This is Bridge Street, which crosses the River Tees using County Bridge. Continue uphill a short way, then turn right at a signpost for Holwick. Immediately on the left is a bridleway sign pointing a way uphill. The bridleway actually runs to the left of the hill-top plantation on Kirkcarrion. We need to trace the line of the Pennine Way, which crosses the ridge well to the right of Kirkcarrion. This is not one of the Pennine Way's most well-blazed parts, but there should be no problem following it uphill. Once through the wall on the ridge, the descent can be a bit fiddly. Aim for a ruined barn, keeping to the left of it. Head downhill for another barn, keeping to the right of it. Across a shallow valley is the farm of

115

Wythes Hill. Despite the number of small fields, all the stiles and gates are in place and the golden rule seems to be to cut diagonally across each field. From Wythes Hill, simply follow the access road down to the B6276. The Pennine Way goes straight across the road and follows an obvious course through fields to reach Grassholme Farm. (Note: old Pennine Way guides show the path running to the left of the farm, but it has been diverted through the farmyard.) Turn left to follow a minor road across Grassholme Bridge. Almost four miles have been walked since Middleton and the Pennine Way is abandoned having got us this far.

The road climbs steeply from Grassholme Bridge. Go through a large iron gate on the left to enter the reservoir enclosure. There is a pleasant shore path which runs between the reservoir shore and the boundary wall. Maps don't show this route and all inflowing becks are bridged. The dam of Grassholme Reservoir is reached in $1^{1}/_{2}$ miles. Follow the access road uphill from the dam, then turn left along a minor road. It is less than $^{1}/_{2}$ mile to a signposted road junction. At this point, on the left, is a footpath signpost. Take careful note of the direction in which the footpath sign points as there is no trodden path across the field. A gate is in view, but it is another gate, downhill and out of sight, which gives access to the next field. Once there, turn left and follow a wall straight down to the bottom of the slope. Go through a gate, cross tiny Eller Beck by a set of slabs, then turn right to go through another gate. Walk uphill to reach Westfield House. Follow the access road away from the house, then turn right to walk down a narrow tarmac road.

A railway viaduct comes into view - a splendid structure built to carry the Tees Valley Railway to Middleton. It has been given a new lease of life as the Tees Valley Way. Walk across the viaduct and continue along the old trackbed. Profusely flowered banks are a delight for almost $^{1}/_{2}$ mile. A sign for Middleton points to the right at a farm. Cross the nearby road at this point and pick up a path which heads towards the River Tees. The river is followed upstream to County Bridge, where the road leads straight back into town.

WALK 24: MIDDLETON, LOW FORCE AND BOWLEES

This is a short and simple walk, suited to those who like to take their time and have a good look at things. The route leaves Middleton and picks up the course of the Pennine Way at County Bridge. This is gentle riverside rambling with no route-finding problems or difficulties underfoot. Pennine Wayfarers and casual strollers rub shoulders alongside the River Tees. The river is left at Low Force, though there is nothing to stop walkers continuing to High Force or even further. Bowlees is close to Low Force and the route is taken that way in order to include the visitor centre, which is really quite interesting. There is also an easy walk up a small beck to Gibson's Cave. This route is left open-ended and it is suggested that a bus can be used to return to Middleton. It is wise to check the times in advance - otherwise arrange to be collected.

Pennine Wayfarers vary considerably. There are those who struggle all the way, oblivious to their surroundings as they wrestle with huge packs and ill-fitting boots. There are those who set themselves incredible daily targets and pound them out relentlessly with their sights fixed firmly on their destination. The River Tees isn't for those people. In fact, it probably isn't really suited to Pennine Wayfarers at all. The Tees is something to be savoured slowly - time and again if necessary. It varies with the seasons and the time has to be just right for the flowery meadows to be fully appreciated. Kingcups, ox-eye daisies, orchids, pignuts and a host of other self-seeding, constantly regenerating species are present. The river itself traces wide, shimmery-silver loops overhung by oak, ash and alder. The bird-life, like the plant-life changes with the seasons and the available food supply. It's rather like walking through an overgrown garden.

Bowlees Visitor Centre is worth an hour or so of anyone's time. The old village school has been converted to house displays and exhibitions which help the visitor to appreciate the unique flora of Teesdale. Notes help with the interpretation of the geology and scenery too. If you're not particularly hot on wild flowers, then a few have been planted and labelled outside. There's also helpful literature which, unlike many general guides, concentrates on Teesdale and deals with specific sites. Just remember to keep an eye on the time if you've a bus to catch to return to Middleton.

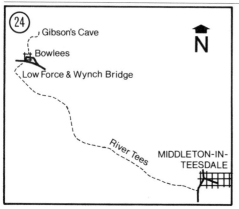

There are only two bridges used to cross the River Tees - one at the start and one at the end. The one at Middleton is called County Bridge as opposite banks of the Tees were in different counties until 1974. The bridge replaced an earlier structure and collapsed while it was being built in 1811. A local butcher had told people that it would fall down and was indicating the bridge's faults to his wife when it happened - killing them both. The other bridge is the slender Wynch Bridge, which is a suspension bridge. This too is a replacement structure. The first bridge was reputed to be the earliest suspension bridge in the country, strung in 1704 by miners intent on easing their journey to work. There is a good view of Low Force from the bridge, but the waterfall is much better appreciated by being viewed from all angles and from both banks. It lacks the power and grandeur of nearby High Force or distant Cauldron Snout, but it owes its formation to the same resistant band of rock - the Whin Sill.

THE ROUTE

Distance:	An easy five mile low-level walk on good paths.
Maps:	1:50,000 Landranger Sheets 91 or 92
	1:25,000 Outdoor Leisure Sheet 31
Start:	Middleton-in-Teesdale
Finish:	Bowlees
Getting There:	Middleton can be reached from Barnard Castle or Alston (B6277), Brough (B6276) or Stanhope (B6278).
Parking:	By the drinking fountain in Middleton.

From the drinking fountain in Middleton, take the road signposted

Low Force near Bowlees

Brough. This is Bridge Street, which crosses the River Tees using County Bridge. Turn right at a Pennine Way signpost and follow a clear track into the fields. The route varies - sometimes a path and sometimes a walled track - but it is always quite obvious throughout. The route starts by running close to a loop in the Tees, then drifts away from it, then settles down to follow it more faithfully. There is a footbridge called Scoberry Bridge, but don't cross it. Continue upstream to Wynch Bridge - a fine suspension footbridge - and cross it. Low Force is only a little way upstream and it is no hardship to study it from both banks. A map is hardly necessary for the walk so far, but it is important to walk up to the B6277 road and not the other way to the Holwick road.

Cross straight over the B6277 and walk into Bowlees. The visitor centre is immediately to hand in an old school and should be spared an hour or so's attention. Leave the visitor centre to walk down to Bow Lee Beck nearby and walk upstream on a good path. This leads to Gibson's Cave which is a charming spot on account of the curtain of water which falls over the opening. Retrace steps to Bowlees to end the walk at the village and wait for the bus to Middleton.

Upper Teesdale is a vast gathering ground for a mighty river. Arctic/alpine plants thrive in this harsh environment, though the natural distribution was spoiled by the construction of the Cow Green Reservoir. The three walks offered don't go *up* the hills, but rather *round* them. The circuit of Cronkley Fell is the most remote, saving High Force for a thrilling finale. On the opposite bank of the Tees is Widdybank Fell, providing a similar habitat for plants, but much easier walking. The circuit of Herdship Fell is accomplished on good, solid tracks, but lacks the floral and scenic highlights of the other two walks. Each walk could be amended slightly to start and finish at the Langdon Beck Youth Hostel.

WALK 25: HOLWICK, CRONKLEY FELL AND HIGH FORCE

This is a long walk, but not particularly hard, though it does get into some rather remote country with no easy exits. A good track leaves Holwick to cross a moor. A partly waymarked path leads towards Cronkley Fell, which is fairly easy to ascend. The descent to the River Tees and the walk alongside the river cross some rough ground, but the going gets better once the Pennine Way is reached. A walk along this well-blazed path leads past High Force - one of the most spectacular waterfalls in the country. Cronkley Fell is often seen by walkers, but not as often visited as Widdybank Fell or Herdship Fell. There is no car park and no easy access, but having said that the walk over Cronkley Fell is one of the best ways to walk over Mickle Fell's sprawling shoulders without actually trespassing there. The huge bulk of the fell is in view and the summit lies about three miles off-route.

Holwick Scar - an outcrop of the Whin Sill near Holwick

Mickle Fell is managed as a vast grouse moor and is also part of the Upper Teesdale National Nature Reserve. While there is no access to the fell, at least the rights of way on the moorland slopes are partly waymarked and walkers aren't discouraged from using them. As grouse moors go this one is particularly well managed and supports a varied population of birds. Apart from the grouse there are curlew, snipe, lapwing, dunlin and redshank to be seen. Black grouse can occasionally be spotted. Birds of prey aren't persecuted, but accepted as part of the scene. High-class shooting parties are entertained at Holwick Lodge - a substantial building which is reputed to have been used by the Queen Mother on her honeymoon.

Cronkley Fell's features are determined by the occurrence of the Whin Sill in this part of Teesdale. The fringe of cliffs overlooking the River Tees are formed of this intrusive rock. This rock type generates a poor, acid moorland cover where it outcrops. It is overlain by a limestone which was baked by the heat of the Whin Sill until its character changed considerably. The limestone actually crystallised and is known as "Sugar Limestone". In appearance it weathers into a coarse gritty soil which is of course abundant in lime. This gives

121

rise to a specific flora which is quite different to the surrounding moors. Unfortunately, it also gives rise to a vegetation cover much preferred by sheep, so steps have been taken to fence off parts of Cronkley Fell to preserve the varied species. The sheep also wear out little sheltering hollows in the easily eroded soil and this has had to be discouraged. Human visitors are few and far between and providing they watch where they are planting their feet there can be no harm in them looking around the enclosures. Far away down the slopes, close to High Force, is a remarkable juniper jungle. Seldom does juniper occur in such profusion and it adopts such strange shapes that it is tempting to believe it has been topiared. The juniper is dominant, but there are quite a few other trees in the same region.

High Force has long been on the tourist itinerary. This is a tremendous waterfall, where the great volume of the Tees suddenly falls and breaks itself over a couple of ledges to create a turbulent scene of boiling, angry water. In times of flood the waterfall cannot be approached from below (by payment to use the path) but from the slopes of Cronkley Fell a safe distance is maintained without losing any sense of its grandeur. The resistant band of rock over which the water pours is the Whin Sill again. Some people like to scramble around the top of the cliff-line, which is fine if you keep an eye on your holds, but there have been a number of accidents there. High Force can't really be explored properly on a single visit, but its proximity to the road means that it can be studied in passing.

THE ROUTE

Distance:	A moderate 12 mile moorland walk with some rough paths.
Maps:	1:50,000 Landranger Sheets 91 or 92
	1:25,000 Outdoor Leisure Sheet 31
Start/Finish:	Holwick
Getting There:	Holwick is reached by a minor road from Middleton-in-Teesdale which is signposted from the B6276.
Parking:	Small spaces in the village.
	Ask permission if in doubt.

Many people walk round Cronkley Fell from the car park at High Force, but Holwick is a quieter place to start and there is a good view

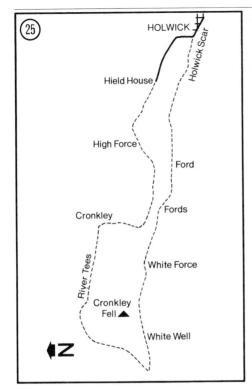

of the impressive cliff-line of Holwick Scar. After parking in Holwick, walk out of the village until the road turns suddenly right. Go left at this point, through a gate at a bridleway sign, to follow a track uphill. Holwick Scar, part of the Whin Sill, peters out and allows the track to climb up to the open moor. Look out for clumps of parsley fern. Little notices indicate other tracks which are out of bounds, so keep to the main track throughout. The bird-life is abundant and provides numerous distractions. Over 1½ miles from Holwick, waymarks point to the right and there is no further access along the track towards Silverband Shop. A couple more waymarks keep walkers on course to Blea Beck, which must be forded. After a descent to ford two more becks, start climbing the variously vegetated patchwork slopes of Cronkley Fell. White Force can be seen off to the left, cutting its way through a narrow defile.

The path levels out over Cronkley Fell and passes a couple of fenced-off areas. These contain sensitive plant sites which have become established on the "Sugar Limestone". As the path starts to descend it passes White Well, where clear water seeps to the surface.

The sugar limestone is very evident here and the water contains much gritty material. It's a wonder this material remains on the fell in the face of the North Pennine elements. The path descends more steeply to reach the bank of the River Tees.

Turn right to follow the Tees downstream. The riverside path can be a bit patchy and in times of flood some parts might be underwater. However, there is plenty of fellside available even if it is rough and steep. After a mile of following the Tees, Widdybank Farm stands on the opposite bank. Teas and snacks can be obtained by anyone who would consider wading across the river. If this option is not taken, continue downstream on easier ground for more than a mile to reach a solitary building. Go through a gate beside it and head straight for a bridge spanning the Tees. Don't cross the bridge, but turn right to follow the Pennine Way along the access track to Cronkley. Go past the farm and climb up the rough fellside beyond. For the next mile the path stays well above the river, then moves down beside it. Try to avoid looking at the ugly quarry on the opposite bank. Heathery fellsides and patches of juniper form an interesting mixture, with Bleabeck Force adding noise and movement. The low rumble of High Force later becomes apparent and a good viewpoint, or series of viewpoints, can be searched out. Stand in silent admiration and let High Force make all the noise as it spills over a cliff of the Whin Sill, breaks over ledges and foams furiously in a wide, wavy pool before rushing onwards through a rocky gorge. This spectacle is witnessed for free from this side. People down below have paid for the privilege.

The Pennine Way continues downstream and leaves the juniper jungle. Don't go down to the riverside, but pass a solitary farmhouse and go through a nearby gate. A track leads past a barn on the way to the farm of Hield House. Follow the farm access road, continue along a minor road and peep at Holwick Lodge on the way to Holwick.

WALK 26: CAULDRON SNOUT AND WIDDYBANK FELL

This is an easy circuit around Widdybank Fell. The route is largely confined to narrow tarmac roads, but these are mostly traffic-free. There is one rough path which is used to descend alongside the impressive cataract of Cauldron Snout. A path which runs downstream alongside the River Tees crosses a sensitive marshy area where duck-boards have been laid to prevent erosion of plant sites. Wandering off-route isn't permitted around Widdybank Fell due to the diversity of species clinging to survival on the fell.

Widdybank Fell's features are determined by the occurrence of the Whin Sill in this part of Teesdale. The fringe of cliffs overlooking the River Tees are formed of this intrusive rock. It generates a poor, acid moorland cover where it outcrops, but it is overlain by a limestone known as "Sugar Limestone" which gives rise to a specific flora quite different from the surrounding moors. For some reason many visitors search for the spring gentian, but there is more to the area than that. A host of arctic/alpines flourish alongside other plants from completely different backgrounds. Mountain pansy, thrift, Alpine bistort, bird's eye primrose, Teesdale violet and blue moor grass is as happy growing here as tormentil, thyme and harebells. Down beside the Tees, Falcon Clints hide other surprises. A few hardy rowans cling to the cliffs, but there was once a greater forest cover which has long been cleared. The woodland plants are still there - including woodland ferns and wood anemones. They have adapted by taking to the shade beneath boulders, or sheltering in rocky crevices. Flowery meadows around Widdybank Farm are quite delightful. Haymaking comes so late in Upper Teesdale that flowers have a chance to drop their seeds before being mown. There is so much to be seen on this circuit that a good handbook should be carried to help with identification.

The siting of Cow Green Reservoir was vigorously opposed and in the end all that could be done in the name of conservation was a massive, last-minute replanting scheme. It is said that even the workmen watched where they were putting their feet. Cow Green Reservoir now offers "amenities" to cater for the visitor and manages to fit into the scene, albeit clumsily.

The resistant Whin Sill causes the River Tees to break into a fury at Cauldron Snout. A series of steps and rocky channels alternatively confine the mighty river then allow it to spread out and break itself into a swirling, foaming and awe-inspiring cataract. The massive concrete dam overtopping Cauldron Snout is an intrusion and it seems unfair that the waterfall owes its impressiveness to a man's

125

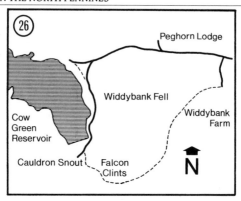

hand on a valve. Only in times of heavy rainfall when the reservoir is filled to capacity can Cauldron Snout truly speak volumes about the sheer power of water, then no man's hand can choke its booming voice.

Falcon Clints, close to Cauldron Snout, takes its name from birds of prey which inhabit it. These were once persecuted, but are now assured of a safe haven. Peregrines might well be noticed. Other more usual moorland birds include grouse, curlew, snipe, lapwing, dunlin and redshank. The existance of Cow Green Reservoir ensures that a number of waterfowl and waders can find at least a temporary reason for stopping in the area. Information boards at the car park at the start of the walk detail something of what might be seen during a visit.

THE ROUTE

Distance:	An easy ten mile moorland walk on paths and roads.
Maps:	1:50,000 Landranger Sheets 91 or 92
	1:25,000 Outdoor Leisure Sheet 31
Start/Finish:	Cow Green Reservoir
Getting There:	Cow Green Reservoir can be reached by minor roads from Langdon Beck or Harwood on the B6277.
Parking:	At the Cow Green Reservoir car park.

Start by studying the information boards at the Cow Green Reservoir car park. These give the bare bones of the geology, scenery, flora and fauna of the area. Follow the nature trail which is signposted nearby. An explanatory leaflet is sometimes available from a box. The nature trail starts off promisingly as a made-up path, but is soon confined to tarmac for over a mile to the foot of the huge, concrete reservoir dam. Outcrops of the unique "Sugar Limestone" can be seen, which allows specialised plants to thrive. Don't cross the road bridge below the dam, but turn left off the road and follow the River Tees a short way to Cauldron Snout.

An easy scramble down rocky steps is required. There is no problem, though it can be a bit slippery when wet and it is wise to stand still while looking at the various parts of the cataract. Powerful displays of creamy-brown water pound against constricting channels of black rock, while a final spill over a stepped pyramid of rock is quite impressive. It seems that the Tees was destined to be a wide river and gets rather annoyed in tight places such as this.

The path moves downstream and is sandwiched between the Tees and Falcon Clints. As the booming voice of Cauldron Snout becomes muted a bouldery area is crossed. Look out for unusual plants in cracks and crevices. A strip of sensitive wetland fills the gap between the Tees and the cliff-line and wooden duck-boards have been laid to protect the area from over-trampling. Some people frown on this as a modern device, but our remote ancestors laid similar structures to cross the Somerset Levels and oaken "toghers" are still unearthed in Irish boglands which were laid in prehistoric times. *They* were trying to keep their feet dry as they bridged treacherous bogs. *We* are trying to preserve irreplaceable habitats. Dry feet are an added bonus.

The cliff-line leans back and becomes less aggressive, while the slope on the opposite bank rears up to form Cronkley Scar. Widdybank Farm comes into view. Teas and snacks are sometimes available, with farming yarns thrown in for good measure if you're lucky. Follow the access road away from the farm through flowery meadows and rougher pastures for over a mile. On reaching a minor road, which some call the Warden's Road, turn left and follow it uphill for nearly 2½ miles. After nearly two miles there are a few old mine workings on the right and later an old brick hut. Simply continue along the road to return quickly and easily to the

127

Cow Green Reservoir car park, enjoying the views of wilderness country all around.

WALK 27: COW GREEN RESERVOIR AND HERDSHIP FELL

Herdship Fell lacks the floral and scenic merits of the other two walks in this section, but it has a quiet, wilderness charm of its own and provides an easy walk on good tracks. There are a number of old mining tracks and other old roads which can be linked to make a circuit of the fell. Wandering over the top quickly leads into rough country, so this is avoided. Anyone who feels inclined to take in the summit will find it is well positioned in Upper Teesdale to afford a good view of the surrounding heights.

There are two sides to Herdship Fell. One is Harwood, seen on the approaches. This is the last fertile part of Upper Teesdale. The other side is the moorland wilderness beyond the Cow Green Reservoir. This has been exploited for lead and abounds in mining remains. The farming community of Harwood is especially striking. Most of the buildings are whitewashed regularly and the doorposts and lintels are painted black. The effect is startling on a sunny day. Legend says that His Lordship was lost on the fell and stumbled across a poor hovel. He was treated kindly and got himself dried and fed. Seeing the condition of his humble tenants, he ordered them to repair their house and send the bill to his estate office. No doubt he was also thinking that in time he could charge a higher rent. His surprise was great when he discovered that the poor farm wasn't even part of his estate. So surprised that he ordered all his properties to be whitewashed so that he wouldn't make the same mistake again!

Cow Green Reservoir was sited in this remote spot to slake the thirst of distant Teeside. Apparently there wasn't another area suitable for drowning. Unfortunately, the area was of immense botanical interest and whatever couldn't be transplanted elsewhere was consigned to the depths. It's an unlikely sheet of water to find in a moorland setting, but it manages to fit into the scene, albeit clumsily. It offers an additional habitat for wildfowl and waders and "amenities" for visitors. It didn't completely slake the thirst of the industrial regions, which simply expanded and demanded

Chapelfell Top and Noon Hill from Cowshill

In the valley of Devil's Water

more. Keilder Reservoir, far to the north, feeds a pipeline which connects with the River Wear and River Tees to boost supplies which can be abstracted later.

A number of old lead mining sites are apparent on this walk. There are crumbling buildings, open shafts, large spoil heaps and sundry other remains and scars. A legacy of this once-flourishing industry is an excellent wide track which allows walkers to penetrate a wilderness area of Upper Teesdale with ease. In fact, the track seems to convey walkers further and further into a remote moorland region, only to leave them on the B6277 wondering where the wilderness went. At a slightly higher level are ski-tows, which serve to remind summer visitors that winter conditions are quite hard in these parts.

THE ROUTE

Distance: An easy ten mile moorland walk on good tracks and roads.

Maps: 1:50,000 Landranger Sheet 91
    1:25,000 Outdoor Leisure Sheet 31

Start/Finish: Cow Green Reservoir.

Getting There: Cow Green Reservoir can be reached by minor roads from Langdon Beck or Harwood on the B6277.

Parking: At the Cow Green Reservoir car park.

Start by studying the information boards at the Cow Green Reservoir car park. These give the bare bones of the geology, scenery, flora and fauna of the area. A track just above the car park is marked "No Entry" but this only applies to vehicles. Start walking along the track, noting evidence of mining almost immediately. Cow Green Reservoir is spread out below. Directly southwards are the expansive moorlands of Mickle Fell. Meldon Hill rises above the opposite shore of the reservoir, while the Dun Fells and Cross Fell are further away to the right. The track itself aims towards Tynehead Fell and after more than a mile of walking a large mining site is reached. Have a poke around the spoil heaps for any good-looking specimens and study the ruined buildings. One building is maintained in a weathertight condition as a shooting hut. Part of the building is left open if shelter is required.

Blanchland Post Office is part of the Abbey gatehouse   129

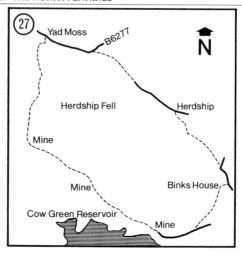

Another mile of walking along this wide, clear track leads to another large mining site. Actually, the track stays above it, but a visit is easily made as part of the walk. The whole area appears to be a vast rabbit warren. If you are looking for good specimens, see what the rabbits have unearthed. There are a further two miles of walking along this track. Mining remains become small-scale and are harder to determine. Grouse, curlew and lapwings might be noticed as the track appears to move further and further into a desolate moorland region. The surroundings are illusory. The track makes a twist and a turn and a short climb brings it against the B6277 road. The wilderness spell is broken suddenly at this point, despite the altitude being around 2,000 feet (600 metres).

Turn right and follow the B6277 for ³/₄ mile. Another right turn reveals an old road which once carried traffic more directly towards Harwood. This is a fairly steep descent and has been abandoned in favour of a gentler course. Walk down the old road, which becomes surfaced with tarmac as it passes Frog Hall and Herdship. At the next building - Watersmeeting - turn right to leave the road and cut across fields to reach a ruined chapel close to Harwood Beck. This decayed structure is potentially dangerous, but it is worth a peep inside. Cross a footbridge over Harwood Beck and walk downstream to reach a road. Turn right to walk up the road, then right again along the access road for Binks House. Yellow waymark arrows point left and show the path leading onto open moorland. The path climbs indistinctly on the moor, passes some small mine workings, then joins a minor road close to a solitary white hut. Turn right to follow the road down to the Cow Green Reservoir car park. If there is any spare time available a short walk down to Cauldron Snout could be considered, but that involves extra miles.

Weardale is still being extensively quarried and there is plenty of evidence of earlier quarries and mines. The dale has also seen extensive use as a hunting forest. The Prince Bishops of Durham seem to have enjoyed the thrill of the chase, with evidence to suggest that the Romans did too. The walks are all quite different. In the lower reaches of the dale the Weardale Way is used to link Wolsingham and Frosterley. An old railway trackbed over the moors is followed from Rookhope to Stanhope. The walk from Westgate is easy and charming, following a delightful river. Chapelfell Top offers hard moorland walking closer to the head of the dale. Throughout Weardale are scenes of beauty and despoilation, but it remains a popular dale and attracts plenty of visitors.

WALK 28: WOLSINGHAM AND FROSTERLEY

The Weardale Way is largely a low-level walk, but between Wolsingham and Frosterley it is routed along the moorland edge overlooking the dale. This is an easy walk on an obvious track. The ascent from Wolsingham is by road and the descent to Frosterley is by road. An easy riverside path is used to complete the circuit. The moorland section offers wide-ranging views over Weardale, while the riverside path allows an intimate appreciation of the Wear itself.

Wolsingham is an interesting little town which is worth looking round. It comes as a surprise to visitors to find a little steelworks here, but basically the town is a Saxon foundation. It has grown to become an impressive market town with several notable buildings - many of which are protected within a conservation area. Some

132

quite substantial buildings surround the triangular market place. On the way out of town is an ancient row called Whitfield Cottages which used to be the Pack Horse Inn. Wolsingham is moderately busy throughout the year, but becomes packed to capacity for the Wolsingham Agricultural Show, which is reputed to be the oldest such gathering in the country. It occurs on the first weekend in September.

Frosterley is largely unremarkable. The village has existed since 1183, but has little to show apart from its quarry-scarred surroundings which account for its fame and fortune. Frosterley Marble is in fact a durable limestone, rather than a true marble. It can be cut and polished to form a quality product. Its coralline character makes it quite distinctive and the polished cross-sections of fossils make each piece an individual study. Frosterley Marble has been quarried for centuries and turns up in a host of monumental settings such as

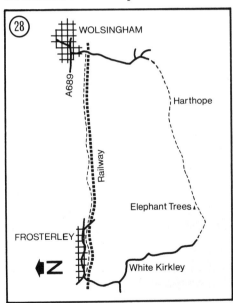

churches, cathedrals (Durham, naturally) and cemeteries. It has also been exported around the world.

Panic reigned in this quiet corner of Weardale in 1745. The much-feared Scots were on the move again and apparently their army was marching across the moors towards the dale. The men of Wolsingham and Frosterley were called to arms by pealing church bells and about a hundred local worthies marched to confront the enemy. But while still some distance away the Weardale men could see themselves to be hopelessly outnumbered and fled. Some time later the Scottish "army" was discovered to be a herd of around two hundred cattle being driven across the moors. Red faces all round, but not the end of animal trouble in this valley. When a police force was established in Wolsingham its first job was to round up a host of wandering pigs and ensure that their owners kept them in stiles or enclosures. It must have been a major operation because the force was substantially reduced once the round-up was completed! Finally, there are the elephants, or rather the Elephant Trees. A small beech copse overlooking this part of Weardale goes by the name of the Elephant Trees as their profile is supposed to resemble elephants on the horizon.

THE ROUTE

Distance:	An easy ten mile walk on paths, tracks and roads.
Maps:	1:50,000 Landranger Sheet 92
	1:25,000 Outdoor Leisure Sheet 31
Start/Finish:	Wolsingham
Getting There:	Wolsingham is on the A689 between Stanhope and Crook.
Parking:	In the centre of Wolsingham.

Leave the centre of Wolsingham by following the main road as if for Stanhope. This passes Whitfield Cottages, which was formerly the Pack Horse Inn. A left turn along the road signposted for Hamsterley Forest leads to a bridge over the River Wear. Climb steeply uphill by road for almost a mile. Bear right along a narrow road marked as "No through road for motor vehicles". This leads uphill a little further, then turns right at an old, overgrown quarry. The tarmac surface becomes patchy and its continuation is a gravel track. Don't follow the track all the way down to the farm of Harthope, but walk straight onwards through a gate to gain access to the open moors. There is a clear track along the edge of the moor which never strays far from a boundary wall on the right.

The track climbs gradually on the heathery moor and passes a small beech copse over 1 ½ miles from Harthope. This feature rejoices in the name of the Elephant Trees as its profile is supposed to resemble them. Less than $1/4$ mile beyond the copse is a track which branches off to the right and runs downhill to Allotment House - a large barn. A narrow tarmac road continues downhill through an oddly wooded area which was obviously once part of a larger plantation. The road leads down to the neat little hamlet of White Kirkley and climbs to a road junction. Old quarries can be seen from the road. Frosterley Marble was taken from these sites and the remains look worthy of exploration. Turn right to follow a road down to cross the River Wear.

Immediately the main road is reached on the outskirts of Frosterley, turn right and walk along a narrow footpath. This offers a back way round the village, passing the Parish Church before joining a patchy tarmac road. Keep right to follow the road gradually down to a railway line. Go through a gate, as if crossing the railway, but turn left without actually crossing it. A short footpath will be revealed which leads onto another little tarmac road. The road appears to run up to the main road, but just before that point is a narrow path beside a row of houses. After passing a scruffy depot, turn right to cross the River Wear by the next road bridge.

After crossing the river, turn left off the road and follow a path which remains between the River Wear and the railway line all the way back to Wolsingham. This is a distance of more than $2^{1}/2$ miles and the path comes in a series of distinct sections. At first there is no access to the actual riverside and several notices are at pains to state this. The riverside is followed closely to get past a caravan site. After following the access road away from the caravan site the path is routed alongside the railway line through a series of fields. End the walk by climbing up to the bridge over the River Wear used at the outset of the walk. Turn left to walk straight back into Wolsingham.

WALK 29: ROOKHOPE AND STANHOPE

A series of disused railway trackbeds and steep inclines are used throughout this walk. On the plus side, this means easy, dry, firm walking surfaces which are clear enough for dodgy navigators to determine with few problems. It is quite a high-level route and crosses exposed moorlands, but the level surface allows walkers to stride out and eat up the miles. The ascent from Rookhope uses an incline, but it isn't excessively steep. The final descent to Stanhope also uses an incline, then takes to the road for the last stretch. As this walk is open-ended some thought needs to be given to transport. Perhaps the easiest way of organising this is to be based at Stanhope, using the scanty bus service to reach Rookhope. The return to Stanhope is then simply a case of walking "home". At 1,670 feet (509 metres) this was the highest standard gauge railway in the country - this height being achieved where the line crosses the flank of Bolt's Law at Redgate Head.

In historical terms, we are actually dealing with two railways. The Stanhope & Tyne Railway was opened in 1834 seemingly in defiance of the contours of the region. Inclines were constructed at Crawleyside and Weatherhill to haul limestone up from Stanhope. Goods were taken along a level moorland line, but there were more inclines on the way to Consett. The railway company was wound up in 1840 with debts of £300,000. The Stockton & Darlington Railway took over the line and had things running again by 1845. At this time the Weardale Iron Company was formed and the Stockton & Darlington Railway was asked to consider constructing a branch line across the moors to Rookhope. It failed to do so, and the ironmasters built the line at their own expense. It joined the existing line at Parkhead, which was also called Blanchland Station. The Rookhope end featured a long incline.

Traffic on the line from Rookhope to Parkhead was never great and gradually dwindled. Closure came by degrees. Practically the last thing to be seen on the line was a battery-powered car in 1925, carrying grouse-shooters in search of sport. The track was lifted in 1943. On the other line, the incline at Crawleyside was abandoned in 1951. The line from the sand quarry at Parkhead lasted until 1968. The only remains outstanding on these old lines are the winding houses, which hauled trucks up and down the inclines. An old boiler from the winding house at Redgate Head, above Rookhope, lies abandoned on the moors half a mile away, for some reason. The workings from the old Weatherhill Engine were ultimately transferred to the National Railway Museum at York.

The terminal points of the walk have some interesting features of note. Rookhope still looks the part of a mining village and there

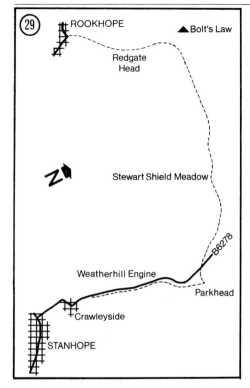

(29) ROOKHOPE
▲ Bolt's Law
Redgate Head
Stewart Shield Meadow
B6278
Weatherhill Engine
Parkhead
Crawleyside
STANHOPE

are indeed working mines further up the dale. The place has a long history, but most of what can be seen belongs to the mining era. Rookhope was chosen as the site of a borehole which finally proved the existence of the Weardale Granite beneath this area. It doesn't outcrop anywhere, so its location had been postulated only.

Stanhope is a fine town and a natural centre for this part of Weardale. When standing in the centre of town, many of the buildings appear to be crenellated - this is fanciful decoration rather than defensive work. Visit the church and study the fossil tree in the graveyard - removed from its moorland site at Edmundbyers Cross. Stanhope Castle, which bankrupted its builder, isn't open to the public, but looks impressive from the outside. The pub called the Bonny Moor Hen was the scene of a riot when miners rescued their comrades from gamekeepers and constables who were holding them there. Their crime - poaching grouse. The event is commemorated in verse.

THE ROUTE

Distance:	An easy nine mile moorland walk on good tracks.
Maps:	1:50,000 Landranger Sheets 87 & 92.
	1:25,000 Pathfinder Sheet 570 &
	Outdoor Leisure Sheet 31.
Start:	Rookhope
Finish:	Stanhope
Getting There:	Rookhope is on a minor road between Stanhope and Allenheads. Stanhope is on the A689 in Weardale.
Parking:	Small spaces in Rookhope. More space in Stanhope.

Start near the post office in Rookhope. Across the road is a footpath sign indicating a track which leads to Hylton Terrace. When the track swings to the right, keep left and continue uphill. The track leads straight out onto a grassy moorland and the incline pursues an obvious course uphill as a wide track. The rocky cutting at the top, called Redgate Head, has the remains of the old winding house and the ruins of cottages which housed workers at this height. This was the highest standard gauge railway in the country at an altitude of 1,670 feet (509 metres). Walk straight through the cutting and follow the level trackbed out onto the heather moors beyond. After a while a sheepfold appears below the track and the old boiler of the Redgate Head winding house lies abandoned there.

As the walk proceeds, look out for a short branch-line on the left which is rather overgrown. Don't follow it as it goes nowhere. There is another track on the left which offers a quick exit to a high moorland road, if required in an emergency. The trackbed continues across the moorland slopes and offers good views over Stanhope Common. There is a road above which is out of sight, but within earshot. The access road for the farm of Stewart Shield Meadow is crossed. A boggy bit of a cutting can be avoided by walking just above it on the right. This is called Wilkinson's Cutting. An embankment leads to the B6278 road near Parkhead. The bridge which once spanned the road has gone, leaving a gap in the line. Don't follow the embankment on the other side of the road, but use a track alongside. This leads to a pile of ugly buildings.

Turn right at the buildings to follow a track. Be careful here as the track is used by heavy quarry lorries. It can also be rather messy.

138

There is no danger from lorries beyond the ruins of the Weatherhill Engine winding house. Notice the neat cottages by the road which once housed the workers here. The incline beyond the Weatherhill Engine runs straight downhill roughly parallel to the road. Boundary stones marked S&DR indicate that the owners were the Stockton & Darlington Railway. There are no obstacles along the way, but it is better to follow the road downhill through Crawleyside and on to Stanhope. If preferred, rights of way can be used to make an exploration of devastated quarried slopes on the way to Stanhope.

Alternative finish. From Parkhead, there is the option of amending this walk by continuing along the Waskerley Way. The link is easily made by referring to Walk 32 from Parkhead. In this way, Stanhope would be abandoned, along with its inclines, and the route would end at Consett instead. Some people do the whole length on bicycles, but there are one or two sections which are a bit rough for all but mountain bikes.

WALK 30: WESTGATE AND MIDDLEHOPE BURN

There is a short, popular and quite scenic walk from the little village of Westgate. In years past this will have been an ugly area, with intensive quarrying and mining taking place. Westgate is left by taking a steep road almost to the high moors. An easy track starts running back downhill and Middlehope Burn is a charming watercourse which leads straight back to Westgate.

Quarrying and mining have long been a feature of Weardale. The enormous Heights Quarry near Westgate is still eating its way into Northgate Fell, but other remains of industry have had their rough edges smoothed by Nature. Tracing the old lead mining structures down Middlehope Burn is rather like finding a lost Inca city, despite the fact that countless visitors have been there already. A series of splendid arches were merely the "bousesteads" where ore was stored before being processed. Little tramways were constructed beside the burn and a number of buildings were erected. All are now overgrown and beautifully embowered in varied woods. The Weardale Iron Company extended a line from Rookhope to Westgate and walkers struggling up the steep road on Scutter Hill should think of the power needed to operate the

Scutterhill Incline. At Westgate itself a more sedate valley railway was constructed as far as Wearhead.

There was a different sort of quarry in the past. The village of Westgate is complimented in name by Eastgate and a search of the map will reveal Northgate Fell. There was no Southgate - just a vast moorland separating Weardale from Teesdale. This part of Weardale was reserved as a hunting forest for the Prince Bishops of Durham. With increasing industrial and agricultural use of the dale it became necessary for the area to be "rudely enclosed with stone of a twelve or fourteen miles in compass" as a sixteenth century writer put it. The "gates" controlled the approaches and a hunting lodge was built in the centre in 1430. The lodge can still be distinguished as a platform with grassy ramparts. The hunting history spans many centuries. A number of Roman altars have been unearthed in the dale and all but one were dedicated to Silvanus - the god of the hunt. One was taken from Rookhope Burn and a replica was cast for the people of Weardale and placed by the road at Eastgate. The inscription was translated as: "Sacred to the unconquered Silvanus, Caius Testius Micianus, prefect of the Sebosian Wing, on account of a boar of unusual size which was captured, which many of his predecessors were unable to take, gladly placed this altar discharging his vow." Stirring stuff, but the Romans were probably in Weardale on account of its reserves of lead, though this is difficult to prove as later workings would tend to obscure any earlier workings. A number of prehistoric caves in the area have yielded the bones of exotic creatures and it seems fair to suggest that the prehistoric people of Weardale also enjoyed the thrill of the chase. It all makes grouse shooting look about as exciting as a game of draughts.

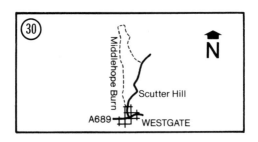

THE ROUTE

Distance: An easy four mile low-level walk on paths, tracks and roads.

Maps: 1:50,000 Landranger Sheets 87 & 92.
1:25,000 Outdoor Leisure Sheet 31 and
Pathfinder Sheet 570.

Start/Finish: Westgate

Getting There: Westgate is on the A689 road between Stanhope
and Nenthead. Also reached by minor road
from Rookhope.

Parking: At a large lay-by just west of Westgate.

Walk back into Westgate from the lay-by and turn left after passing the post office/Co-op. The road climbs very steeply past a series of quarries. After climbing for a mile there is a wide, walled track on the left. Follow this gradually downhill past the ruin of a farmhouse at Shield Close. After a short walk uphill a gate on the left is where a path leads down to Middlehope Burn. Turn left at the bottom and simply follow the burn back down to Westgate.

The route-finding is simple and leaves the walker free to contemplate the old lead mining remains. Tramways were built to serve the mines and all sorts of structures can be determined by the observant on the way downstream. On the natural front, the spoil heaps are being colonised by spring sandwort, a rare plant which has a particular liking for poisonous lead wastes. The woodland which is confined to the narrow part of the lower dale is called Slit Wood and is quite ancient. The woodland floor supports a variety of shade-loving plants such as ramsons, wood sorrel, bluebells and wood anemones. Hard outcrops of rock cause Middlehope Burn to feature charming little waterfalls. Water power was used at the mining sites and an old mill will be noticed on entering Westgate at the end of the walk. The mill wheel has gone, though the wheel pit remains and the garden is profusely flowered.

WALKING IN THE NORTH PENNINES

WALK 31: ST. JOHN'S CHAPEL AND CHAPELFELL TOP

There is a vast moorland crest separating Weardale from Teesdale which is crossed by minor roads touching 2,000 feet (600 metres). It is wild and inhospitable country and largely untrodden. Good tracks from St. John's Chapel and Ireshopeburn allow an easy ascent and descent, but the actual high moorlands are quite stern. However, Chapelfell Top and Noon Hill are rather easier to visit than some of the other parts of this wilderness. The higher parts of this walk are quite difficult and this makes it suitable only for fine weather. In poor weather it would be an energy-sapping trek and there could be problems with navigation on the unmarked sections. At Ireshopeburn there is an opportunity to visit the Weardale Museum of High House Chapel.

Following the Reformation the Prince Bishops of Durham lost some of their status and property and were disinclined to hunt in Weardale. The ancient hunting forest fell into disrepair and the game either perished or fled. The Church was still entitled to a tithe on all the lead mined in the dale and certain clergy were so wealthy that they were largely absent and left their affairs in the hands of their curates. There were many reasons why the dalesfolk distrusted the established Church and Upper Weardale was almost completely Presbyterian at one point. When John Wesley visited the area and preached by the waysides he aroused considerable interest. He was welcomed throughout the Pennines and seems to have had a special affection for the region. On one trek over from Teesdale he noted that "from the top of an enormous mountain we had a view of Weardale. It is a lovely prospect; the green, gently rising meadows and fields, on both sides of the little river as clear as crystal, were sprinkled all over with innumerable little houses." Surely the mountain was Chapelfell Top - perhaps not the actual summit, but some point on the flank. On the route offered there is a stone in the shape of a chair which offers just such a prospect.

Wesley preached at Ireshopeburn between 1750 and 1790 from a corner marked by a memorial. The Weardale Museum is directly opposite, situated in the minister's house at the High House Chapel. The chapel was built in 1760 and is the second oldest Methodist chapel still in use. The museum is entirely a local venture and is divided into a number of sections. Having won a Carnegie "Interpret

142

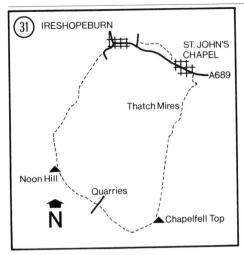

Britain" award, you can be sure it's worth a visit. The Wesley Room is devoted to exploring the influence of John Wesley on this part of the world. The rest of the exhibits and displays offer insights into the life, work, landscape and history of Weardale.

Ireshopeburn and St. John's Chapel are linked by a low-level section of the Weardale Way at the end of the day. Also running between the two villages is an old railway trackbed. This was the Weardale Extension Railway, which was built along the length of the dale and reached Wearhead in 1895. The only remaining part of the railway is in use as an industrial line as far as Eastgate. St. John's Chapel is largely noted for its cattle mart - the pens are seen close to the Golden Lion at the start of the walk.

THE ROUTE

Distance:	A difficult seven mile moorland walk with no paths on top.
Maps:	1:50,000 Landranger Sheet 92
	1:25,000 Outdoor Leisure Sheet 31
Start/Finish:	St. John's Chapel.
Getting There:	St. John's Chapel is on the A689 between Stanhope and Nenthead. Also reached by minor road from Langdon Beck.
Parking:	At St. John's Chapel.

There is a small church dedicated to St. John in St. John's Chapel. A bridleway signpost points across the main road at that place and indicates a walled track rising behind the Golden Lion. This track is easy to follow and it zig-zags uphill past the old farmhouse of Thatch Mires. Another broad track is joined and followed by turning right. Open moorland is finally reached at a gate. Abandon the track at this point and head straight uphill, aiming for the corner of a wall on the skyline. There is a level patch of wet moorland beyond, then the slope continues rising. This is completely untrodden country and a mess of peat hags and groughs are encountered before a tottery cairn is reached. This can be said to mark the 2,306 feet (703 metres) summit even if it isn't quite on the highest bit of ground. The summit is 2½ miles up from St. John's Chapel.

Clear weather is helpful for the descent as there are no features to follow across the moors. There is a boundary ditch which runs to Fendrith Hill, but don't be drawn along this. By taking a compass bearing along the line of the district boundary, a very scanty line of rotting fencepost stumps might be found. These are a poor guide on the moor, but the idea is to get to the top of the minor road at Harthope Head, which shouldn't be too difficult. The road runs as high as 2,056 feet (627 metres). Be careful not to be drawn too close to quarries which have eaten into the moors.

From the highest part of the Harthope road, follow a fence on the far side which guards the edge of a deep quarry. A rotting line of old fenceposts continues in the same direction - roughly north-westwards - to reach the unremarkable summit of Noon Hill. This is only slightly higher than the Harthope road and is marked by a stout fencepost where the district boundary makes a right-angled turn left. To leave the summit of Noon Hill, turn right at the solitary fencepost. The shape of the moorland doesn't allow a view of the descent until later. Once there is a view down the slope, head for an old railway van parked at the end of a walled track. The track offers an easy descent to Ireshopeburn and is surfaced with a distracting array of minerals from Weardale's old lead mines. Rich pickings are available for anyone wanting to start a collection.

Ireshopeburn is finally reached by road and passed through by turning right along the A689 road. Continue as far as the Weardale Museum of High House Chapel - to which a visit is recommended. To continue the walk, turn left off the main road at the Museum and cross the River Wear by the road bridge. Turn right to follow the river downstream on a good path. Walk past the first footbridge, which isn't required, and walk further downstream. Keep to the left of a building, then turn right to cross a footbridge over the river. After walking under a disused railway, turn left to walk back into St. John's Chapel along the main road.

Derwentdale Section

Derwentdale is noted for places such as Blanchland and Edmundbyers, or the enormous Derwent Reservoir between them. The Waskerley Way is included in this section as it has a foot in Derwentdale, but it could be started from Stanhope and therefore be included as a Weardale walk. The walks over the moors from Edmundbyers and Blanchland are quite popular, but are sometimes walked in forms slightly different to those offered here. The walk in the valley of Devil's Water is included here simply for want of somewhere to put it. It isn't really a part of Derwentdale and wouldn't be at home in the Allendale section either.

WALK 32: THE WASKERLEY WAY

The Waskerley Way is a clearly blazed route which follows an old railway trackbed across the moors. This keeps to a level from Parkhead to Waskerley, then loses height on a long incline. The route leaves the North Pennines altogether and heads for the former steelworks town of Consett. Signposts only admit to this being the Waskerley Way between Waskerley and Consett, but there should be little difficulty with route-finding even in poor weather. It is a good route to consider for a rainy day as the surface of the old trackbed is firm throughout.

Purists might well want to walk this old line from Stanhope in deference to history, as the inclines between Stanhope and Parkhead were part of the same line. These are covered in Walk 29 and by combining the two walks it is possible to stride out a long way on quite an easy route. The Stanhope & Tyne Railway was opened in

1834 seemingly in defiance of the contours of the region. Inclines were constructed at Crawleyside and Weatherhill to haul limestone up from Stanhope. Goods were taken along a level moorland line, then inclines were used to lower trucks downhill from Waskerley. On the way to Consett, Hownes Gill was crossed by means of two inclines - one down into the gill and one up the other side. It meant that traffic was slow moving. The Stanhope & Tyne Railway was wound up in 1840 with debts of £300,000. The Stockton & Darlington Railway took over the line and had things running again by 1845. A passenger service operated along the length of the line, but only Waskerley was offered as a destination from Consett by 1847. The Weardale Iron Company built a linking line from Rookhope to Parkhead. Parkhead became known as Blanchland Station. Waskerley was built up as an entire railway village with an engine shed, repair shop, housing for the workers as well as a school and chapel. Burnhill had a minor station and Rowley had another. All the stations have been demolished, though anyone wanting to see Rowley Station are directed to Beamish. The station was rebuilt as part of the vast open-air museum to show an example of a typical country station. The steep incline down from Waskerley, called Nanny Mayor's Incline, was cut out with the construction of a less severe detour. The inclines at Hownes Gill were replaced with a splendid viaduct leading straight to Consett. This structure is 730 feet (220 metres) long and its maximum height is 150 feet (45 metres). Its construction consumed 2½ million bricks. The inclines above Stanhope were abandoned in 1951. The rest of the line functioned until 1968, when the closure of the steelworks at Consett sealed its fate.

With the lifting of the track and the demolition of many features of the old line, there is little to see in the way of remains. The trackbed, however, is perfectly clear and in places has been equipped with car parks and picnic sites. Durham County Council has been praised many times for converting its old railway network into walkways and heritage routes for public enjoyment. Consett is getting rather distant from the North Pennines, but the route is taken all the way there because it lies at the centre of a series of converted trackbeds. Apart from the Waskerley Way, which offers a route from Derwentdale to Weardale, other routes radiating from

Consett offer destinations as diverse as Durham, Sunderland or Newcastle. Long distance walkers who are also railway buffs might be interested in making further explorations. (See also *Walking Northern Railways*, Vol 1, East by C.Emett. Cicerone Press.)

THE ROUTE

Distance:	An easy ten mile moorland walk on good tracks.
Maps:	1:50,000 Landranger Sheets 87 & 88
	1:25,000 Pathfinder Sheet 571
Start:	Parkhead
Finish:	Consett
Getting There:	Parkhead is on the B6278 between Stanhope and Edmundbyers. Consett can be reached from Wolsingham, Edmundbyers, Durham or Newcastle, as well as many other places.
Parking:	By the roadside at Parkhead. Also at Waskerley, White Hall, Rowley and Consett.

Parkhead is nearly three miles up the B6278 from Stanhope and is easily recognised by its huge, ugly sheds. The place is also marked by having an old railway embankment on either side of the road. Walk towards the ugly buildings and turn left along another track. A gate gives access to open moorlands. The scenery improves greatly, but isn't exactly spectacular. The trackbed is clear to follow throughout and Waskerley Reservoir lies some distance below it. Simply stride out and eat up the miles, disregarding any farm or reservoir access roads which cross the line. Closer to Waskerley there are gates to open and close. As Waskerley is the only village passed on these high moorlands it cannot be mistaken. It is reached four miles into the walk.

Beyond Waskerley the trackbed leads to a forested area, then makes a sudden dog's leg turn to the left. (The continuation, which is private, is an old line running to Tow Law.) Walk through a cutting lavishly lined with clumps of broom. There is a blockage to be by-passed where the bridge giving access to Red House has been replaced by an earthen bank. After the cutting, a wide, grassy embankment fringed with rowans and hawthorns continues gently downhill. Views back towards Waskerley feature the course of

148

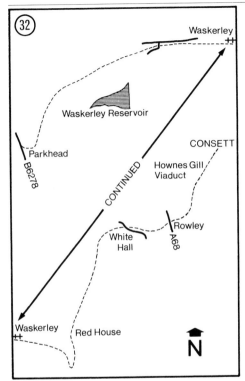

Nanny Mayor's Incline. The two lines meet close to a minor road at White Hall, where a car park has been provided. Just before this point is a cutting lined with broom and heather which is quite attractive.

Continue along the trackbed from White Hall to Rowley. There is another car park and picnic site at Rowley. The old station was demolished and has been rebuilt at Beamish, the large open-air museum. The A68 has to be crossed and the trackbed continues to Hownes Gill Viaduct. Walk straight across the top of the viaduct, which gives fine views over Hownes Gill itself - a charmingly wooded dale. The viaduct can only be appreciated properly by climbing down the valley and studying it from below. This is an option for anyone with time to spare. The trackbed continues a little further, but it is necessary to enter Consett by road to end the walk. This isn't a particularly attractive place and it seems remote from the North Pennines, but other trackbeds radiate from the town and lead to places such as Durham, Sunderland or Newcastle.

149

WALK 33: EDMUNDBYERS AND EDMUNDBYERS COMMON

The outward and return sections of this walk are seldom more than ¼ mile apart, certainly never as much as ½ mile, but they are as different as chalk and cheese. The outward journey uses a series of farm tracks to climb gradually up to high moorlands. Only at the very end is heather moorland really apparent. The return journey is almost entirely across the moors and only softens into pastoral country quite close to Edmundbyers. This is quite easy walking on good tracks, but there is a short section which could be awkward to follow in poor visibility. There is also little shelter on the high moors, though in bad weather the farm tracks could be used for the return journey.

Edmundbyers is a quiet little village in a gentle part of Derwentdale fringing the higher parts of the North Pennines. There is an interesting church, a pub, shop, Youth Hostel, farms and other buildings fringing a wide green. St. Edmund's Church surely has no real connection with St. Edmund, King and Martyr, but it is worth a visit on account of its features of interest. There may be items of Saxon stonework incorporated into the structure and there is certainly Norman work, but the building has been ruthlessly restored. The altar is of a single slab of stone - a type forbidden in 1571, when it was removed according to instructions and replaced. It wasn't destroyed, but simply buried and came to light again in 1855. It has been restored to its original use.

The Youth Hostel might well serve as a base for walkers exploring Derwentdale and the building is worthy of inspection. It was built in 1600 and was known as the Low House Inn. It stood at a strategic crossroads between Tynedale, Weardale and Allendale. The inn finally lost its licence, but courtesy of the YHA accommodation, if not ale, is still available. The interior is quite homely and is reputed to be haunted by the ghost of a former landlord who died of exposure while searching the moors for his wife, who had gone missing.

The farms passed on the way to the higher moors- College, Pedam's Oak and Belmount - are all derelict, but were once buildings of some character. There has been a farm at Pedham's Oak since 1380 and the place takes its name from a horse-thief who hid in a rotten oak trunk near that site. The scene changes from sheep

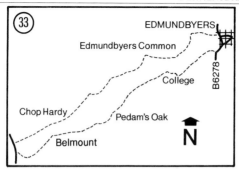

pastures to heather moorlands managed for grouse shooting, but lead mining is never far away in the North Pennines. On the higher parts of the walk a couple of chimneys come into view which were linked by flues to smelt mills over in Ramshaw. The dale is rather too far away to include in the walk and its devastated nature isn't at all apparent. In fine weather there are good views over Northumberland from the highest parts of the route. Anyone with time and energy to spare could enhance the views by climbing to the 1,771 feet (540 metres) summit of Bolt's Law.

THE ROUTE

Distance:	An easy nine mile moorland walk on good paths and tracks.
Maps:	1:50,000 Landranger Sheet 87
	1:25,000 Pathfinder Sheets 561, 570 & 571
Start/Finish:	Edmundbyers
Getting There:	Edmundbyers is on the B6278 between Consett and Stanhope. It can also be reached by the B6306 from Hexham.
Parking:	Spaces around Edmundbyers.

Leave Edmundbyers by following the B6278 road as if for Stanhope. Go past the churchyard (opportunity for a visit) and continue downhill. Take the track on the right at a sharp left bend before reaching the bridge over Burnhope Burn. Don't walk up to the farm on this track, but keep left to cross a slope of gorse and bracken. After

151

more than $1/2$ mile there is a right turn where a good track leads up past the derelict farm of College. In a mile the track passes through the farmyard at Pedam's Oak, which is another derelict farm. The track descends a little, then climbs through fields to get to a third derelict farm - Belmount - a mile from Pedam's Oak. Keep above Belmount to pick up a track which follows a wall gently uphill on rougher moorlands. Drift gradually to the right on the track to reach a minor road at 1,444 feet (440 metres). About four miles have been walked to this point and the views all round are quite good, with the most distant taking in parts of Northumberland. Closer to hand is the heathery expanse of Bolt's Law and a couple of smelt mill chimneys which carried poisonous fumes up from Ramshaw.

Turn right to follow the road a short way to a public bridleway signpost, then turn right again to step back onto the moor. The way ahead is rather vague at first, but keep an eye peeled for evidence of a trodden way and a good path and track will appear as if by magic. This leads to a series of shooting butts by a gate. Go through the gate and continue walking gradually downhill following the widest track across the moor. Another gate takes the track from the heather moorland to a predominantly grassy moorland. Yet another gate takes the track back onto the heather moorland. Follow a broad, grassy track across the moors and continue descending gradually. There is a pronounced bend in the track where it crosses a burn, then the route keeps below an isolated field system. The track crosses another burn and finally leads back into Edmundbyers. If the church of St. Edmund's wasn't visited at the outset, it can be found down a minor road on the right immediately on re-entering the village.

WALK 34: BLANCHLAND AND BLANCHLAND MOOR

Blanchland is beautiful - a term seldom used for North Pennine settlements, which are often rather stern-faced. It can be fairly busy and quite a few people might be noticed heading for the moors above. The walk is easy in its outward section, but a bit awkward on the return. The outward journey is basically a clear track over Blanchland Moor which goes on through Slaley Forest. The return journey uses an old pack-horse track called the Carrier's Way. This is quite popular, but it is largely buried in the heather and can't be hurried. There could be route-finding problems in poor visibility, especially where the Carrier's Way is abandoned for a direct route down to Baybridge. On a fine day the route is a delight and there is much of interest.

Blanchland is dominated by its Abbey Church. It appears to be haphazardly designed in a curious "L" shape with a tower which seems rather stout. There's a story behind it all which spans many centuries. The Abbey was founded in 1165 by Premonstratensians and the name was certainly recorded as Blanchland in 1214. In the fourteenth century the Abbey was crowned with its fine tower. After Dissolution in the sixteenth century the Abbey and its lands came to the Radcliffe family, then to the Forster family. After plundering for stone and other building materials, the only place of worship was a little chapel built roughly where the current Abbey entrance is. In 1699 Lord Crewe, the Bishop of Durham, married into the Forster family and ultimately came to hold the Abbey estates. When he died in 1721 he left it all in the care of trustees, who built the present Abbey Church by filling in the gaps between the most upstanding parts of the ruins. Thus it became "L" shaped. Most of the rebuilding took place in 1752 and several interesting items of stonework are preserved inside. It's as good as a museum, but the Abbey Church is only half of the story.

The village of Blanchland is largely based on the plan of the Abbey's outbuildings. The large gatehouse, which now houses the post office, was used by the lay brethren to enter and leave the Abbey. The Abbot's lodge is now the Lord Crewe Arms and its most notable feature is a huge fireplace. The lawns at the back of the Lord Crewe Arms are the remains of the Cloister and Chapter House. The large, gravelled village courtyard is surrounded by restored cottages which were once the refectory, dormitories and workshops of the brethren.

Locally mined lead had the silver extracted on site. There are plenty of other features around the village which aren't associated with the Abbey. The old school has a pair of pillars which once carried the winding gear at the Ramshaw lead mines. A charming old pigsty is located by the riverside.

While on the walk, a large lead mine site is passed fairly early at

Shildon. This is in a dangerous condition and shouldn't be approached. Miners and drovers were in the habit of stopping at Pennypie House, high on the moors, where pies were dispensed for a penny apiece. Slaley Forest is one of the few large forests in the North Pennines. Only the fringe of the plantation is entered, and then only for a brief mile. It isn't as varied as Hamsterley Forest, but it attracts its share of visitors. The walk along the Carrier's Way overlooks the valley of Devil's Water, which is one of the least visited dales in the North Pennines.

THE ROUTE

Distance:	A moderate nine mile moorland walk on paths and tracks.
Maps:	1:50,000 Landranger Sheet 87
	1:25,000 Pathfinder Sheet 560
Start/Finish:	Blanchland
Getting There:	Blanchland is on the B6306 between Edmundbyers and Hexham. It can also be reached from Rookhope and Stanhope.
Parking:	At a car park at Blanchland.

Blanchland is so interesting that it would be ridiculous to go there simply for the walk described, so have a good look around first, then head out of the village by way of the car park. Continue along the tarmac road, which is replaced by a gravel track beyond Shildon. Note the old lead smelt mill chimney, but keep well away from the ruins which are in an unsafe state. The track continues to Pennypie House, over 1¼ miles from Blanchland, where a gate gives access to the moors beyond. The track climbs rather more steeply to gain open views across the moorlands fringing this part of the North Pennines. A level walk is followed by a gentle descent to the edge of Slaley Forest, about two miles from Pennypie House. The track enters the forest and the route stays close to its edge for a mile.

Upon entering the forest, turn left along a track which cuts through a clear-felled and newly-planted area. The track runs into a taller, mature stand. The moment the track starts swinging to the right, look out for a path which follows a forest ride on the left and leaves the forest by a gate. The track appears to forge straight across

154

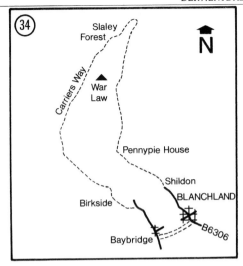

the moors, but bear slightly to the left of it to walk gently uphill. Locate a hollow way and follow this to a gate in a fence. Go through the gate.

The hollow way is covered in heather, but features a very narrow trodden path throughout. This is the Carrier's Way and has obviously seen much greater traffic in the past. Walk along it and check off the following features to mark progress. A large shed will be noticed below the track, close to a point where another track cuts across at right-angles. Walk straight through this junction and follow the Carrier's Way further around the hill. Good views look into the valley of Devil's Water. A gentle walk downhill leads to a gate in a wall. Go through the gate and continue along the track to a solitary wooden post. Turn left and walk gently uphill past another post. A grassy way across the heather leads to a gate. A stony track is picked up at this point and leads off the moors. When this rough surface ends abruptly, turn right and walk down to the farm of Birkside. Follow the access road away from the farm, then turn right to walk steeply down to the little village of Baybridge by road.

At Baybridge, walk towards the bridge over the River Derwent.

There are two options available for a return to Blanchland. The map shows a footpath (actually a wide track) running through the woods above the southern bank of the river. There is also a path which isn't marked on the map which follows the northern bank of the river. Both routes measure ¹/₂ mile. Riverside rambling is therefore on offer by turning left without crossing the bridge. Woodland walking is on offer by turning left after crossing the bridge. Once back at Blanchland, the village can be inspected once more - it is just as interesting a second time around.

WALK 35: DEVIL'S WATER AND HANGMAN HILL

There is a little-known and little-visited dale in the North Pennines drained by Devil's Water. There is a remote hill tucked out of sight at its headwaters called Hangman Hill. It all sounds very sinister and macabre, but this turns out to be gentle and unremarkable country. It would be wrong to omit this area entirely, yet there isn't enough walking to justify devoting a whole section to the dale. The single walk offered fills the yawning gap between Derwentdale and Allendale. In truth, the walk around Lilswood Moor is just as much a part of Hexhamshire Common as Walk 37 in the Allendale section. However, I've put it in with the Derwentdale section as it seems to have more affinities in that direction than the other.

Perhaps the main reason for Devil's Water being so often by-passed is because it is served by a spider's web of minor roads. The first part of the journey involves careful navigation through the network to locate the starting point. The walk is fairly short and straight forward, but a crossroads of little-trodden bridleways at Hangman Hill can be rather confusing. Clear weather would be a distinct advantage on the circuit.

Was there ever a gibbet at the remote crossroads at Hangman Hill? It would certainly have been a handy place for one to be sited - handy for the surrounding dalesfolk to reach while remaining distant enough so as not to trouble their consciences. Whatever slender thread the truth hangs on, you wouldn't want your party to become too strung out in case some of them swung too far off-route and got cut down in bad weather - then you might get it in the neck!

THE ROUTE

Distance:	A moderate seven mile moorland walk on paths, tracks and roads.
Maps:	1:50,000 Landranger Sheet 87
	1:25,000 Pathfinder Sheet 560
Start/Finish:	Broadwell House
Getting There:	Broadwell House is almost at the end of a network of minor roads reached by way of Hexham and Whitley Chapel.
Parking:	Beside the phone box opposite Broadwell House.

Parking is very tight at the start of this walk and the only really useful spot is beside the phone box opposite Broadwell House. Follow the road signposted for Harwood Shield. This road climbs uphill for nearly ³/₄ mile to reach open moorland, then descends for nearly a mile to reach the remote farmstead of Harwood Shield. Just as the last building is reached, turn right off the road to follow a good track roughly parallel to a burn. The track passes a couple of railway carriage shelters, then ahead it can be seen to split and climb up either side of a prominent, steep-sided little valley. Branch to the right and cross the headwaters of Stobbylea Burn. It is tempting to want to follow a broad track uphill, but in fact you need to trace a sparsely cairned line along the edge of the steep-sided little valley.

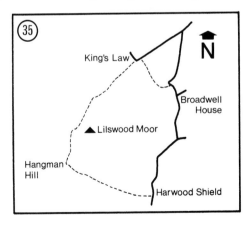

A couple of posts with arrows later define the route more clearly. Keep an eye on the map and the ground to be sure of reaching a point where two bridleways cross. This looks very simple on the map, but neither of the routes is particularly well trodden and a grouse-shooter's track slashes straight through the junction. The successful completion of the route hangs (pardon the pun) on making the right choice on Hangman Hill. Be sure to follow the bridleway which runs northwards across the flank of Lilswood Moor.

The way ahead isn't very clear at first, but becomes much better with distance. There are wide-ranging views as height is gained - looking across Hadrian's Wall country to the distant Cheviot Hills. A boulder painted with a white arrow marks a bend to the right, but this is quite clear without such an aid. A long, gradual descent ends with the track splitting into a number of grooves and ridges, but they all lead to the corner of a minor road close to a stand of trees.

Cross a cattle grid on the road, then go through a gateway on the right. There is a right of way which forges straight across to a lower road, but it isn't trodden underfoot and can be a bit awkward to trace. It leaves the first road at right angles and crosses fields before descending to a small burn in $1/2$ mile. After crossing the burn it continues down to the lower road at a gateway. Turn right and follow the road uphill to the phone box opposite Broadwell House.

There are two Allendales - the East and the West - and Allendale Town is the only sizeable settlement. Try and make a visit on New Year's Eve, when the Allendale Fire Festival features costumed "Guisers" carrying blazing tar barrels on their heads to a central bonfire. The surrounding moorlands don't rise to particularly great heights, but they are wide-open and offer good walking. Many walkers concentrate on the River Allen itself, which furnishes a number of gentle strolls. A firm favourite is Allen Banks and Plankey Mill, with a network of interesting, easy, woodland paths. Hexhamshire Common is blessed with a number of bridleways. The Allenmill Flue offers a definite feature to follow from the river to the high moors. The walk in the West Allen is based on the Youth Hostel near Ninebanks, climbs to a high viewpoint and takes a look at an old highway.

WALK 36: ALLEN BANKS AND PLANKEY MILL

The network of short walks by Allen Banks and Plankey Mill seem to be everyone's favourite. Mixed woodlands are situated on steep, craggy slopes which confine the River Allen to a bouldery bed. There are plenty of paths available and the route offered here explores the course of the River Allen from Ridley Hall to Plankey Mill. There is a detour uphill to Morralee Tarn at the start and an optional climb to the "Bone Floor" viewpoint towards the end. This is easy walking in delightful surroundings and offers a suitable tour in all weathers.

The former walled garden of Ridley Hall has been converted

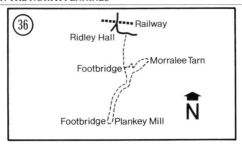

into a car park and picnic area. This, and the wooded gorge are all under National Trust control. The estate covers nearly 200 acres and is the only sizeable property held by the Trust in the North Pennines. Perhaps land suitable for the Trust never comes up for sale, perhaps the near-feudal system of land ownership prevents the Trust getting a foothold in the region. Whatever the reason, they are notably absent throughout the North Pennines.

The River Allen flows through a gorge containing a great variety of trees and infinite nuances of light and shade allow a host of plants to thrive. Garlicky ramsons are a feature of early summer and water lilies later cover the surface of Morralee Tarn. The tarn is artificial and could do with a clean-out as it is only half its original size. Autumn is the most colourful season, bringing a riot of green and gold to the scene. Damp places are colonised by delicate ferns, mosses and fungi. Squirrels might be noticed, while wood warblers and dippers can be seen in their respective elements of wood and water. The power of the river was once harnessed at Plankey Mill, which is the only part of the walk outside of National Trust control.

THE ROUTE

Distance:	An easy four mile woodland walk on good paths.
Maps:	1:50,000 Landranger Sheets 86 or 87
	1:25,000 Pathfinder Sheets 546 & 547
Start/Finish:	Ridley Hall
Getting There:	Ridley Hall and Allen Banks are signposted from the A69 between Haltwhistle and Haydon Bridge.
Parking:	There is a car park close to Ridley Hall.

Suspension footbridge over the River Allen at Plankey Mill

Killhope Wheel - centrepiece of the Lead Mining Centre

Moorland wilderness near Nag's Head

On the way to Melmerby Fell

The car park for Allen Banks is in the former walled garden of Ridley Hall, but there is no access to the Hall itself. A large information board details the main paths available and notes points of interest. Follow the path behind the board and follow the River Allen upstream through the woods. Cross a narrow suspension bridge within $1/2$ mile, then go straight up a flight of stone steps. A path leads uphill through oaks and beeches, waymarked with white-ringed posts or stones carved with the word TARN. The path eventually gains Morralee Tarn, which is embowered in larch and Scots pine. In the right season the surface features a cover of water lilies.

A wide path continues uphill past the tarn, then starts to descend towards the river. There are all sorts of options, but try to follow a good terrace path upstream, gradually descending to the River Allen. Leave the woods and walk through a flowery meadow, passing a riverside ruin on the way to Plankey Mill. Cross over a suspension bridge and start following the river downstream. Either remain fairly close to the river to return to the car park, or take a left turn first to visit the "Bone Floor" viewpoint. This name refers to the sheepbones which have been used as a rather macabre surfacing material. The detour to the viewpoint makes the walk slightly longer than stated, but not much.

WALK 37: ALLENDALE TOWN AND HEXHAMSHIRE COMMON

Hexhamshire Common is a huge, heathery quarter of the North Pennines. It is bounded by Allendale and Devil's Water. While it is largely preserved for grouse-shooting it is also criss-crossed by a network of bridleways. There are no villages and only a few farms confined to sheltered, shallow valleys. Practically the whole of Hexhamshire Common stands above 1,000 feet (300 metres) but no point reaches 2,000 feet (600 metres). The effect is of a vast, undulating heather moor. The walk takes in a couple of bridleways within easy reach of Allendale Town. The first one is clear and easy to follow, but the second one is less distinct and needs care in poor visibility. The return to Allendale Town uses a riverside path from Sinderhope which is gentle throughout. Walkers interested in making longer

161

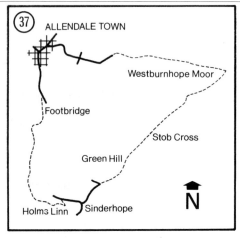

walks on Hexhamshire Common could follow Broad Way, which runs roughly from Allenheads to Whitley Chapel. The only problem for a day walker is arranging some sort of pick-up at the end of the walk. The arrangement of bridleways would also allow a lengthy zig-zag expedition to be undertaken by hardier walkers, which would be a fine way of exploring this seldom-trodden region.

There are few features of outstanding merit along the walk, but Allendale Town's many pubs are surely worthy of note. Walkers might like to reserve their walking in this place until New Year's Eve - locally known as Old Year's Night. The Allendale Fire Festival, or "Tar Barling" takes place as one year gives way to another and has done for as long as anyone cares to remember. A visitor chancing upon the town would be able to appreciate why there are so many pubs, but would have considerable difficulty getting to the bar of any of them. Historians have hotly debated how long the festival has been taking place, but the Allendonians simply get on with things. In recent years people have drifted in from Tyneside and parking has become quite a problem. Apart from drinking, the rough plan of the evening begins with the arrival of costumed "Guisers" and a small band. Towards Midnight the Guisers pick up their sawn-off barrels, which are filled with combustibles and when they are all in lines the barrels are put to the torch. The procession moves around the town headed by a man carrying a long pole with a fire at one end. They walk as a river of fire to every road leaving town, then return to the main square and heave their barrels onto a large bonfire - as near the stroke of midnight as possible. Cheers drown out the ringing of church bells and the drinking goes on. It would be wrong to assume that the drinking was that important, as the locals, on the whole, tend to drift away within an hour, leaving bewildered visitors wondering what happens next. Nothing happens - life goes on and the Allendonians believe that their community will never die while they are able to raise their unique flame.

THE ROUTE

Distance:	A moderate ten mile moorland walk with an easier finish.
Maps:	1:50,000 Landranger Sheet 87
	1:25,000 Pathfinder Sheet 560
Start/Finish:	Allendale Town
Getting There:	Allendale Town is on the B6295 between Haydon Bridge and Upper Weardale. Also reached by minor roads.
Parking:	Around the central square in town.

Leave Allendale Town as if for Haydon Bridge, but turn off the road at a school to follow Shilburn Road as it twists and turns to the outskirts of town. It straightens out and makes a bee-line towards the higher moors. the tarmac surface ends after $1^1/4$ miles and a gate gives access to the open moors at a signpost for Hexhamshire. The first part of the moorland track is an awkward series of grooves and ridges, but it quickly gains a better surface and proceeds more clearly uphill. Wide, heathery moorlands above 1,200 feet (350 metres) are crossed. Views are expansive, but otherwise unremarkable. The track features a few marker posts to keep walkers on course where grouse-shooter's paths might cause confusion. A gentle descent leads to a green hut positioned by a wall.

Don't go through the wall, but turn right to follow it roughly south-westwards across the moors. Note the large farm of Westburnhope situated in the valley below. There is a vague path

163

which runs roughly parallel to the wall, but it later drifts away from the wall to run across open moorland. A bulldozed track crosses this path, but don't be tempted to follow it as it wanders off our course. The path continues indistinctly across an area of bare ground with ditches and stones. A solitary post at Stob Cross marks the point at which our route crosses another bridleway. Keep walking roughly south-westwards, aiming to the left of a tree-capped rise called Green Hill. A wall deflects walkers downhill to a gate, bringing to an end 4¹/₄ miles of moorland wandering over the Common.

A walled track leads downhill from the gate and a narrow road continues the descent to the B6295 at Sinderhope. Turn right at Sinderhope and follow the road past a disused Methodist chapel. A little further away, on the left, a footpath signpost reveals a steeply zig-zagging path leading down to the charming waterfall of Holms Linn. Cross the River East Allen by a footbridge at this point, then turn right to follow a waymarked path downstream. The river banks are attractively wooded in places and the path passes through a number of fields. There is a messy farmyard at Park, then a wide bridge will be noticed further downstream. Don't cross the bridge, but walk further downstream to reach a narrow footbridge close to a crumbling cliff. Cross the river at this point and walk up to the B6295. The riverside walk measures two miles and a ³/₄ mile road walk returns to Allendale Town and its many pubs.

WALK 38: ALLENDALE TOWN AND THE
ALLENMILL FLUES

The flues from the Allenmill smelt mill can be traced for 3¹/₂ miles as they climb 820 feet (250 metres) from the River East Allen to the high moors. Following them makes an interesting day's walk from Allendale Town. A riverside path leads down to Allenmill. A lack of rights of way on the lower slopes means that a zig-zagging route has to be followed which crosses the flue from time to time. The final mile or so is routed alongside the flues and at this point they are quite well preserved. With care, the features of the flue can be studied in some detail. Be careful, as the stonework is often loose and some parts have caved in. There are other flues in the North

Pennines, but the Allenmill flues are the best preserved and should really be consolidated before they are lost for ever.

Effective and economic lead smelting was a science and the smelt-men were a well-educated class. The process of smelting was basically something anyone could manage - heating the ore sufficiently to drive off the sulphur and leave the molten metal. Too much fuel or too little air made the process wasteful and uneconomic. As smelt mills became more efficient they also became larger. The attendant pollution became a problem in the dales as sulphurous fumes blighted people's health and lives. In 1778 Bishop Watson pressed for the introduction of long flues to enable fumes to be carried far from the dales to be expelled from chimneys on the high moors. Construction of the flues was of course expensive, but they ensured a healthier environment. There was an added bonus - as the fumes travelled along the flues they cooled and deposits accumulated along the stone walls. These were formed of sulphur, droplets of lead and other substances which would otherwise have been lost. Young lads were employed to scrape these deposits from the flues and these were subjected to further refinement. No doubt this was a less than beneficial experience for the lads, but everyone else was happy. The Allenmill flues feature a wide "flume chamber" in their most well preserved parts, with entrances every so often to allow the accumulated deposits to be brought out.

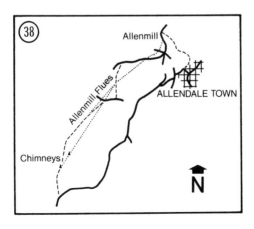

Allendale Town's many pubs are worthy of note. Walkers might like to reserve their walking in this place until New Year's Eve - locally known as Old Year's Night. See introduction to Walk 37.

THE ROUTE

Distance:	An easy eight mile walk on good paths, tracks and roads.
Maps:	1:50,000 Landranger Sheets 86 or 87
	1:25,000 Pathfinder Sheet 560
Start/Finish:	Allendale Town
Getting There:	Allendale Town is on the B6295 between Haydon Bridge and Upper Weardale.
	Also reached by minor roads.
Parking:	Around the central square in town.

Leave Allendale Town via the Whitfield road, but don't follow the road all the way down to the bridge over the river. A signpost right for Allenmill indicates a riverside path running downstream alongside the River East Allen. There are a number of ruins to remind visitors that this was once a working river. After walking almost a mile, cross the river by a road bridge and walk past Allen Mill. The mill is still an industrial site, though lead smelting has long ceased. The flues which end on the high moors started here, but their ruins are lost in ivy. The road continues past the mill to reach Thornley Gate. Five roads radiate at this point - take the one signposted for Ninebanks. The road climbs past a golf course and it is just possible to determine where the flues cut across, though they can't be followed. Keep walking uphill and take the second track on the left. This is a gravel track which crosses the flues and allows them to be studied properly for the first time. They can be distinguished in the view as they head for the moors to two ruined chimneys. The track continues to a minor road. Turn right along the road, then left to follow a farm access road which runs uphill between the two flues.

There have already been opportunities to study the structure of the flues, but the final mile of uphill walking traces one of the flues exactly. Don't be tempted to walk inside the flume chamber, or on top of it, as the drystone structure is in a poor state. By all means peer inside and imagine the hot fumes rushing through. There are a

166

couple of bricked-up archways which allowed access for the young lads employed to scrape down the walls every so often. It is easy to imagine their working conditions, though only fine traces of sulphurous deposits remain. There are two ruined chimneys on the higher moors. The taller one is actually on the line of the other, more ruinous flue. Walk across to it, then walk towards the other chimney stump. Archways at the foot of the chimneys show how the flues connected.

There are two options to end this walk and both are the same length. Either retrace steps back down the line of the flue, looking a second time at the best parts, or continue a short way across the moor to reach a minor road. A left turn along the road allows a rapid descent to Allendale Town. Either way, Allendale Town and its many pubs are the ultimate destination.

WALK 39: NINEBANKS AND HARD RIGG

The single walk offered here serves as an introduction to West Allendale. The short circuit is based on Ninebanks Youth Hostel, which is some distance from the village of Ninebanks. A road and track head for the open moors, but the rest of the ascent is over untrodden ground which could pose route-finding problems in poor visibility. Hard Rigg isn't one of the North Pennines' most noted heights, but if offers a good all-round view. The descent cuts across to a wide track at Long Cross and offers an obvious line back down towards Ninebanks.

In the summer months there are plenty of coaches and cars carrying tourists along the A686 - the Geordie short-cut to the Lake District. The main road offers a good view over West Allendale, but few travellers seem to be drawn into the network of minor roads which branch and branch again until some of them become tracks to the open moors. The route of the highway from Alston to West Allendale has altered over the years and the map readily reveals a dead straight line which was one of the earlier routes. Another route went over by way of Long Cross and this is included in the walk. The main road seems the most obvious way in and out of West Allendale, but motorists should consider using the minor road which goes over to Nenthead, which allows a fuller appreciation of the dale.

West Allendale above Ninebanks

There are no large settlements in West Allendale and Ninebanks comes in two small parts - one part where most of the people live and the other part clustered around the Parish Church. The rest of the population live in a series of scattered hamlets and farms. The higher buildings tend to be derelict, though a few have been rescued from final collapse. Ninebanks Youth Hostel is a part of the scattered community of Mohope, where a couple of old buildings have had their fall into ruination arrested. There is a small, homely old lead miner's cottage which the YHA took over. An adjacent building was adapted as a family annexe and also housed visiting groups. The hostel was proposed for closure in 1991, but the decision was subsequently reversed. This was great news and the hostel will continue to attract many people to West Allendale who wouldn't otherwise have come. It is incumbent upon walkers to support the Hostel at Ninebanks. There is a danger that the North Pennines will eventually be left with only the Pennine Way Hostels. These have the most up-to-date facilities but are often populated by Pennine

Wayfarers looking for a cheap doss. The hype associated with the Pennine Way attracts many people who will never walk another route in their lives and somehow complete the journey on grumble-power alone. Better to be sat in front of a real fire with kindred spirits at Ninebanks than to share a hostel with such malcontents. To give the YHA their due, they have initiated one of their "Camping Barn" schemes in the North Pennines, offering basic accommodation in Teesdale and Weardale.

THE ROUTE

Distance:	A moderate six mile moorland walk with some good tracks.
Maps:	1:50,000 Landranger Sheets 86 or 87
	1:25,000 Pathfinder Sheets 559 & 569
Start/Finish:	Ninebanks Youth Hostel
Getting There:	Ninebanks and the Youth Hostel are signposted from the A686 between Alston and Haydon Bridge.
Parking:	Extremely tight - see below.

Parking is extremely tight at the start of this walk. Patrons of the Youth Hostel have a small space, but others would need to stop almost ¹/₂ mile beforehand, where a prominent track branches from the road. There is space for a vehicle there, but it would have to be parked neatly at the side. From whatever parking space is used,

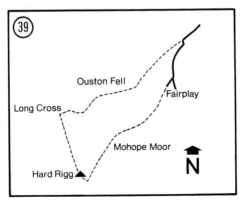

169

The Youth Hostel at Ninebanks - an old miner's cottage

continue along the minor road past the Youth Hostel. Take the next road on the right after ¼ mile and walk uphill almost to Fairplay. A gate on the left gives access to a track, which is later confined between walls. The track passes a stand of trees which almost obscures the ruins of Mohope Head from view. A gate at the end of the track leads onto the grassy Mohope Moor.

The summit of Hard Rigg is 1½ miles away, but the way forwards isn't too obvious. Resist the temptation to turn right and follow wheel marks uphill. Rather, head only slightly to the right to proceed. There are a series of grassy grooves across the moor- the remains of an old pathway which the moorland is reclaiming for its own. Follow this line, vague as it is, in a roughly south-westward direction, then keep to that line when the path finally disappears. The crest of the moorland will be gained at a wall and by turning right the summit trig point will be reached on Hard Rigg at 1,791 feet (546 metres). It is a definite feature to aim for in this region of wiry grasses and rushes. The view takes in the Cross Fell range and continues through Black Fell to Cold Fell. Whitfield Moor spreads its bulk to the north and is crowned by a conspicuous stone hut. The view down Allendale continues to the distant Cheviot Hills. A peep over the wall reveals the highest buildings of Alston.

The wall running over the summit of Hard Rigg marks the boundary betwen Northumberland and Cumbria. Follow it roughly northwards to descend to the corner of a forest, then continue along the edge of the forest to cross a heathery patch of moor. A wide track is reached at Long Cross close to a series of shooting butts. Turn right to follow the track for 2½ miles down to a minor road. It descends slightly to cross a small burn by a railway sleeper bridge. A short ascent leads to a level area of moor, then a gate is reached. The rest of the track goes straight downhill between enclosing walls and seems to point straight towards the little spired church at Ninebanks. The road is reached well before the church. If your car is parked here, then the walk is over. If it is parked at the Youth Hostel, then simply turn right and walk along the road to end the walk.

Daleheads Section

The daleheads of the Allen, Wear and Nent are huddled together at the heart of the North Pennines. The counties of Cumbria, Durham and Northumberland meet in the same desolate area. This guide ends here, but many walkers would do well to start here by looking around the Heritage Centres at Allenheads, Killhope and Nenthead. It is useful to know something about the life and work of the area and each centre offers information in this respect. The three walks overlap slightly. The Allenheads walk is based on a large loop which occurs at the end of the Weardale Way and therefore explores two dale heads. Killhope Wheel is so interesting that it is tempting to forgo the walk over Killhope Law. The walk from Nenthead rubs shoulders with that from Killhope at the point where the North Pennine counties of Cumbria, Durham and Northumberland meet.

WALK 40: ALLENHEADS AND COWSHILL

The Weardale Way ends in a large loop which takes in Cowshill, Killhope and Allenheads, returning to Cowshill. I suggest walking this loop in the opposite direction and using Allenheads as the start and finish of the walk. The route leaves Allenheads by road so that the village can be studied. A moorland track known as the Carrier's Way is used to cross over to Killhope. Killhope Wheel Lead Mining Centre is an obvious distraction, but I would suggest saving an exploration until later and get straight onto the riverside path to Cowshill. An easy track and road crosses the moors to return to Allenheads.

Allenheads was a major centre for the Blackett-Beaumont family concern - which became known as WB Lead. The family took

172

mining leases as early as 1696 and held them for two centuries, thus allowing a continuity and stability to reign in the local enterprise. Vast amounts of lead were extracted and a record-breaking silver nugget of 12,000 ounces was discovered. Allenheads Hall, once the family's summer residence, is now used as a classy shooting lodge. A smelt mill at the foot of the Carrier's Way at Allenheads is now in ruins, but it dealt with lead from Killhope and the surrounding area.

Allenheads had fallen upon hard times in recent years, then suddenly shook itself and undertook a major redevelopment. The Allenheads Heritage Centre is the place to start. A ruinous seventeenth century inn has been converted into a multi-purpose building which houses the village store, a community centre, conference centre and holiday accommodation. Interesting displays outline the history of the village with reference to old photographs and records. Across a courtyard planted with flowers and ornamented with a fountain is the Hemmel coffee shop, set at one end of a converted byre. The North Pennines AONB Officer has an office at the other end. In a separate building is an Armstrong hydraulic engine which was built in 1846 and supplied Allenheads with electricity. After a couple of moves it was noticed at an auction and has been returned to its original home. It has been restored to working order and provides power for the Heritage Centre.

The rest of the village has seen a few redevelopments. There is an old Blacksmith's Shop which was used until the 1960's before falling derelict. It has been restored and the same building houses exhibits which describe the mining and wildlife of the area, with reference books available for use. An environmental centre and nature trail have been established. A trout farm and craft shops are in operation. Mention must be made of the Allenheads Inn, built in 1770, which has weathered the passing of time and continues to serve ale and provide accommodation. The interior is rather like a museum, containing assorted bygone relics. Allenheads deserves a rousing cheer for what it has done. The interested visitor can be accommodated and fed, educated and entertained, and enjoy themselves on wonderful moorland walks - all due to the efforts of a community which decided against stagnation and rose to the challenge of revitalising itself.

THE ROUTE

Distance: A moderate 11 mile moorland walk, broken by an easy section.

Maps: 1:50,000 Landranger Sheet 87
                 1:25,000 Outdoor Leisure Sheet 31

Start/Finish: Allenheads

Getting There: Allenheads is on the B6295 between Allendale Town and Upper Weardale. Can also be reached by minor roads.

Parking: At the Heritage Centre car park in Allenheads.

Walk down through Allenheads from the Heritage Centre. It is almost a mile to the road signposted Alston. Cross a road bridge at this point and turn left to go through a gate by a public bridleway signpost. Walk straight uphill from the ruins of an old smelt mill and pick up a wide track known as the Carrier's Way. This is

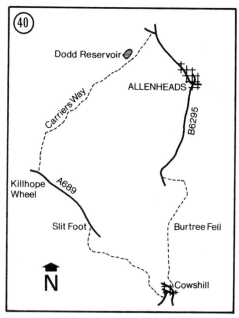

accompanied by a collapsed flue which carried poisonous fumes to be expelled on the high moors. The Carrier's Way is quite clear and climbs past Dodd Reservoir, which will be noticed in retrospect. The track actually terminates at a couple of open shelters quite close to the summit of Killhope Law, but shouldn't be followed so far. About 1¾ miles up from the road, turn left at a small marker post to walk across moors reaching 2,050 feet (625 metres). There are a couple of other marker posts to look out for in poor visibility. The path starts running downhill to a forest. A muddy track through the forest completes the descent to the A689. Turn left and try not to be drawn into the Killhope Wheel Lead Mining Centre - save that for Walk 41.

Follow the main road down-dale for a mile to Slit Foot. A footpath signpost on the right is the start of the descent to Killhope Burn. Go through the roadside gate, then turn left to go through another gate. Drift gradually across stony ground to descend to the riverside. There is a bridge at this point, but don't cross it. Walk downstream and cross the next bridge. The path tends to drift a little away from the river, then climbs quite high above it, but a track later conveys walkers back down to the riverside. Continue downstream to reach a road bridge, then turn left to cross it and walk up to Cowshill. Turn right at the first road junction to reach the Cowshill Hotel, then turn left uphill at the Hotel. Only a short way up the road is a bridleway signpost on the right.

The bridleway from Cowshill runs quite plainly uphill to regain the high moors. It passes a farm, then a building cluttered by old vehicles. The track surface becomes less well defined, but there is always a wall or fence alongside which gives the main direction. The crest of the moorland is reached at 1,950 feet (595 metres) 1³/₄ miles up from Cowshill. A waymark beside a gate shows the way off the moor - turning left to follow a wall downhill for over ¹/₄ mile. The B6295 road has been evident, but a little distant, throughout the ascent on the moor. Now it is joined at a small green gate and by turning right a 1¹/₂ mile walk downhill allows a quick return to Allenheads and its remarkable Heritage Centre.

WALK 41: KILLHOPE WHEEL AND KILLHOPE LAW

Killhope Wheel Lead Mining Centre can prove to be a great distraction and as the hours slip away the time available for tackling a walk over Killhope Law becomes less. Strict discipline is required. Have a look at the rough layout of the Centre, then do the walk, returning later to undertake a more detailed exploration. There is a short forest trail which is a good warm-up for the walk and this is included in the total mileage. The Carrier's Way is an old track used to gain the high moors, but it is rather spoilt as it has been used for forestry operations. Killhope Law is gained by a fairly easy walk, but the continuation to the main road at Killhope Cross is quite difficult and boggy. Killhope Law is obviously highly regarded as it bears a large cairn and a tall wooden mast. A romantic local poet credited the hill with the power of speech, but perhaps that is going a little too far.

The half-mile forest trail at the Lead Mining Centre is quite ingenious. The first part of the walk visits a small hillside reservoir and information boards show how water was brought many miles in special channels to be used at Killhope. Sluices controlled the flow and the power of the water operated the machinery at the mills. The second part of the walk features site reconstructions in forest clearings. The development of lead mining in the sixteenth and eighteenth centuries is demonstrated. The trees keep everything separate and concentrate the mind wonderfully.

Killhope Wheel is the obvious centrepiece of the site and makes it one of the most exciting lead mining museums in the country. Wainwright's Pennine Way Companion lamented that so many old lead mines were falling into ruins and asked that "some enlightened local or public authority in the north, should acquire, restore and preserve a typical specimen lead mine as a site museum for the future benefit of engineering students or even the general public". He concluded gloomily "Alas, it is too much to ask. Nothing will be done." In recent years there has been a great interest in these sites and Killhope Wheel Lead Mining Centre is pre-eminent among them. The wheel itself is over 33 feet (10 metres) in diameter and powered a crushing mill. Ore came from the Park Level, whose entrance can be seen on site. The bousesteads and washing floor have been restored and equipped with authentic-looking workings. This is a hands-on museum where the exhibits are there to be used. All the buildings have been restored to their original use and the mine shop is one of the most absorbing structures. The downstairs has a smithy and stables. Upstairs is a reconstruction of the sleeping quarters. These are quite primitive, but no indication can be given of the true conditions, which were grossly overcrowded, filthy, damp and smelly. Ill health was prevalent and miners died young.

DALEHEADS SECTION

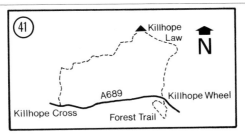

Some local farmers worked in the mine and some of the miners worked on the surrounding farms. One person at least is known to have trekked in every week from Hexham.

Ore from Park Level was taken over the Carrier's Way by pack-horses and smelted near Allenheads. When the Allenheads mill closed the ore had to be taken to the Allenmill works near Allendale Town. Transport was hardly efficient. The last place which smelted ore from Killhope was over at Rookhope. By the time the railway reached nearby Wearhead in 1895, the lead-mining years were practically over. Killhope Wheel was subjected to decay, ruin and vandalism before being rescued from the brink of oblivion.

THE ROUTE

Distance:	A difficult six mile moorland walk with an easy start.
Maps:	1:50,000 Landranger Sheet 86 or 87
	1:25,000 Outdoor Leisure Sheet 31
Start/Finish:	Killhope Wheel
Getting There:	Killhope Wheel is on the A689 between Nenthead and Stanhope.
Parking:	At Killhope Wheel car park.

Killhope Wheel Lead Mining Centre is very interesting and well worth a thorough exploration. I'd suggest a quick look around, including the forest trail, then set off in earnest towards Killhope Law. Leave the car park by walking across the ford in Killhope Burn. Go through a gate into the forest across the main road. A forest track runs uphill and is rather muddy. A vague path crosses the moor above the forest. This is the Carrier's Way and it is marked by a

177

couple of posts. Follow the path for no more than $^1/_4$ mile, then swing left across grass and heather to aim straight for the summit of Killhope Law. There is a trig point at 2,207 feet (673 metres), but attention is more likely to be drawn to a substantial cairn and a 30 feet (10 metres) high wooden mast. These structures help to identify Killhope Law from afar. Views are extensive, featuring the Cross Fell range and a surprising peep over to the Lake District. In the same way the eye is led far beyond the Allendales to the Cheviot Hills. The great bulk of Mickle Fell lies southwards. The walk so far has been relatively easy, covering only $1^1/_2$ miles since leaving Killhope Wheel. The easiest descent is simply to retrace steps, but there is a tougher stretch of walking available to Killhope Cross.

A ditch is aligned to the Durham and Northumberland county boundary and this is the key to continuing the walk. The ditch is fairly clear at first, but zig-zags alarmingly through all points of the compass. It is sometimes filled with squelchy moss and later disappears in a messy area of peat hags and groughs. This can be very difficult country in bad weather, with only the odd wooden post or rotting stump to identify the course of the county boundary. Cloudberries grow in this desolate area. The worst bogs come to an end at the point where the counties of Durham, Northumberland and Cumbria meet. There is a small cairn there and a few beaters for putting out a moorland fire, if you happen to find one in this sodden waste.

To leave the moors, follow a fence roughly southwards, which leads straight down to the A689 at Killhope Cross. There is a stone cross by the wayside, but attention is more likely to be distracted by huge boundary signs. The altitude of the road at Killhope Cross is 2,056 feet (627 metres) and this makes it the highest classified road in the country. About $2^1/_4$ miles of rough country have been walked since Killhope Law, but the return to Killhope Wheel is an easy $1^3/_4$ miles down the road. The rest of the day can be spent admiring the Lead Mining Centre in some detail, using the many exhibits, and perhaps enjoying a meal in the restaurant attached to the Visitor Centre.

WALK 42: NENTHEAD AND NAG'S HEAD

This walk leaves Nenthead and passes its Heritage Centre. A wide track leads quickly to the high moors - to a charming spot called Perry's Dam, which is backed by a view of Cross Fell. A climb onto Nag's Head is followed by a walk across some boggy ground, but there is a good guide in the form of fences and walls. The walk crosses the high road at Killhope Cross, then heads straight back onto the moors. After visiting the point where the counties of Cumbria, Durham and Northumberland meet, the route makes a quick exit from the moors. A clear track is used to descend rapidly back to Nenthead. This is mostly fairly straight forward walking, but the boggy nature of the higher moors can make it hard.

Nenthead is largely a planned village, but it looks rather haphazardly laid out. A large smelt mill was built by Colonel Liddel in 1738, but he couldn't get enough ore through it for it to be economical. He sold the whole enterprise to the London Lead Company. The "Quaker Company" had enough mines to keep the mill well supplied. The benevolence of the company gave Nenthead a couple of social "firsts". This was the earliest place to have compulsory education and a school was built for two hundred children in 1818. In 1833 the first free library in the country was built. The company quickly gained a loyal workforce through their provision of such schemes. There are plenty of substantial old buildings to be seen on a tour of the village, but there is a general air of neglect and much has already been lost. A Heritage Centre has been raised from the near-total dereliction of the old smelt mill site. The Assay House is the most complete structure, with others being restored. A collapsed flue leads up to a chimney on the moors which for some years has been bent at such an angle that it seems in imminent danger of tumbling. The agent for the company's North Pennine lead mines had a house at Nenthead and visitors who have been to the other great company town of Middleton-in-Teesdale will notice the twin of the black and yellow painted cast-iron memorial drinking fountain to Robert Bainbridge. This is rather shabby at Nenthead and the fountain-head is certainly less impressive.

The Vielle Montagne Company moved in around the turn of the century to continue where the "Quaker Company" left off. There

179

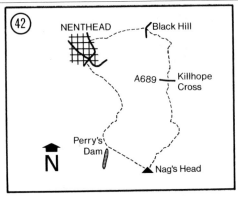

are buildings on the smelt mill site known as the "Barracks" which housed foreign workers. Part of the village centre was cleared to provide a site for a five storey gravity mill which could handle huge quantities of ore. The remnants of the mill now serve as a depot for Wright Brothers, who run the local transport system. The company was started by Mrs Wright in 1914 with only a pony and trap. Her sons continued the enterprise, which still offers routes through some of the most forbidding and thinly populated regions.

THE ROUTE

Distance: A difficult six mile moorland walk with an easy start and end.

Maps: 1:50,000 Landranger Sheets 86 or 87
                 1:25,000 Outdoor Leisure Sheet 31

Start/Finish: Nenthead

Getting There: Nenthead is on the A689 between Alston and Upper Weardale. Can also be reached by minor roads.

Parking: Between Nenthead and Overwater.

Start between Nenthead and the adjacent hamlet of Overwater. There is a car park for the Heritage Centre there, with an information board which tells of the early years of Nenthead. Walk along a road which quickly becomes a gravel track as it moves upstream to the Heritage Centre. Continue uphill on a broad track which passes a

180

small reservoir which will be noticed in retrospect. The track later crosses the headwaters of the Nent at a large building and is followed further uphill past a series of small waterfalls. The small reservoir of Perry's Dam will be reached, 1³/₄ miles from Nenthead. The Cross Fell range is prominent in the view beyond.

A ruined wall and fence run uphill from Perry's Dam to reach Nag's Head. It is furnished with shooting butts and offers a faultless guide to reach the moorland crest at 2,207 feet (673 metres). Turn left to follow the wall and fence which are aligned to the Cumbria and Durham county boundary. This traverses some 1¹/₂ miles of rough, boggy moorland, but again offers a faultless guide despite the nature of the ground. The A689 is reached at Killhope Cross. There is a stone cross by the wayside, but attention is likely to be distracted by huge boundary signs. The altitude of the road at Killhope Cross is 2,056 feet (627 metres) and this makes it the highest classified road in the country. Cross straight over the road and follow a fence up the moorland slope for ¹/₂ mile. This leads to a point where the counties of Cumbria, Durham and Northumberland meet. There is a small cairn there and a few beaters for putting out a moorland fire, if you happen to find one in this sodden waste. Follow the fence as it bears left and runs downhill for another ¹/₂ mile. This ends at a minor road at 1,999 feet (609 metres). Cross straight over and follow a walled track straight downhill for nearly a mile to reach the top end of Nenthead. There are all sorts of ways to complete the little remaining distance to the car park. Wander round the village and note the many buildings of substance and character.

Long Distance Walks

There is no doubt that long distance walkers can really appreciate what the North Pennines are all about. The best routes are long through routes, where one dale gives way to another and one moorland crest is followed by another. Backpackers are able to be quite flexible in their itineraries, taking advantage of high, wild sites (though technically they should ask permission). Hostellers are largely limited to using the Pennine Way Hostels, though Ninebanks and Edmundbyers lie within walking range of the rest. Each of the long distance walks are offered in outline only. The longer walks can be sampled and the lie of the land studied by using the appropriate day-walks listed alongside.

There are various approaches to long distance walking. Some people like a well-blazed and well-publicised route and the Pennine Way would suit them well. Others are content with quiet, low-level routes which have all their gates and signposts in place. The Weardale Way and Teesdale Way would be the most suitable for them. Hardy walkers and fellrunners prefer a stiff challenge - try the Teesdale Watershed Walk, but don't expect to enjoy it. Another high-level wilderness walk traces the imaginary line of the main Pennine Watershed through the region. Walkers who prefer a strong built-in theme to a long distance walking route could try linking a series of old railway trackbeds and combine this with a bit of historical research.

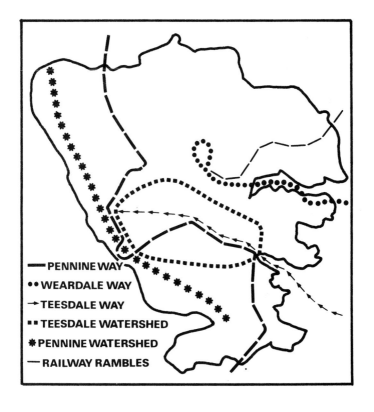

PENNINE WAY

•• WEARDALE WAY

→ TEESDALE WAY

▪▪ TEESDALE WATERSHED

✳ PENNINE WATERSHED

— RAILWAY RAMBLES

1: THE PENNINE WAY

In its totality the Pennine Way runs from Edale, in Derbyshire, to Kirk Yetholm, in the Scottish borders. The North Pennine section covers 62 miles, from the A66 to Lambley. It has served to introduce many thousands of walkers to the North Pennines and takes a fairly good course through the region.

Bowes Moor, Baldersdale and Lunedale become progressively more scenic, then the route reaches beautiful Teesdale. Easy riverside rambling culminates in the spectacular waterfalls of Low Force, High Force and Cauldron Snout. A dreary and exposed moorland crossing becomes suddenly exciting as High Cup breaks into the view. An easy descent leads to the charming red sandstone village of Dufton. A lengthy ascent of Knock Fell is followed by a walk over the Dun Fells to reach the mighty Cross Fell. A prominent mining track, once an old corpse road, offers a direct and clear descent to Garrigill. Gentle riverside rambling leads to Alston, then the route becomes rather dull - sometimes using the riverside and sometimes routed along the course of the Maiden Way. Uninspiring moorlands are faced on the way to the Tyne gap.

(Parts of the Pennine Way can be sampled on the following walks: 4, 5, 6, 10, 11, 17, 18, 23, 24, 25, & 26.)

2: THE WEARDALE WAY

The Weardale Way traces the River Wear from the North Sea to the head of Weardale, ending with a loop which actually takes it over to Allendale. Weardale features some active quarries which are quite an eyesore, but there is plenty of beauty too. The Weardale Way is generally a low-level route, but from time to time it reaches the moorland fringes of the dale. Its final section is over quite high moorlands. The walk is fairly well waymarked. The North Pennine section of the route covers 34 miles.

The Weardale Way passes high above Wolsingham and has good views over the dale. After drifting down to Frosterley the River Wear is followed from time to time via Stanhope and Eastgate. There is a choice of high and low-level routes between Eastgate and Westgate. The Weardale Way links St. John's Chapel, Ireshopeburn, Wearhead and Cowshill. The final loop from Cowshill uses the high-level Carrier's Way to cross from Killhope Wheel to Allenheads, then returns to Cowshill.

(Parts of the Weardale Way can be sampled on the following walks: 28, 30, 31, 40 & 41.)

3: THE TEESDALE WAY

The Teesdale Way is rather like the Weardale Way. It follows the River Tees from the North Sea into Upper Teesdale. The North Pennine section of the route could measure up to 35 miles as the route incorporates variations. The footpaths which make up the route are well waymarked throughout. Teesdale is especially beautiful and has some of the finest waterfalls in the country.

Wooded pathways lead upstream from Barnard Castle and the River Tees itself lies in a channel which is deeply entrenched in the surrounding countryside. The villages of Cotherstone and Romaldkirk are charming and lie within easy reach of the river on the way to Middleton-in-Teesdale. Easy riverside rambling culminates in the spectacular waterfalls of Low Force, High Force and Cauldron Snout. There are no rights of way available to take the walk to the source of the river, so Cow Green Reservoir is the most practicable end to the walk.

(Parts of the Teesdale Way can be sampled on the following walks: 19, 20, 24, 25 & 26.)

4: THE TEESDALE WATERSHED WALK

This is an ambitious challenge route for super-fit, competent navigators. The route appeared as an article in the April 1977 edition of *Climber & Rambler*, but it was postulated before that time. This is a 49 mile walk based on Middleton-in-Teesdale and is routed around the watershed of the River Tees. This is very rough and remote country, highly exposed in bad weather, with access problems in many parts. To make it even more difficult, a 30 hour time limit is suggested. This isn't an enjoyable walk, but the simple fact that a challenge has been issued is enough for some hardy folk to want to do it.

The walk leaves Middleton-in-Teesdale, crossing Harter Fell and Bink Moss to reach the vast spread of Mickle Fell. Little Fell, Murton Fell and Backstone Edge lead to Knock Fell. A fairly easy walk along the Pennine Way leads over the Dun Fells to Cross Fell, then it's back to the wilderness. Round Hill and Tynehead Fell are crossed before a road is reached at Yad Moss. Burnhope Seat, Coldberry End and Three Pikes give way to another road. Chapelfell Top and Fendrith Hill are crossed before a final road is reached. A tough stretch of walking over Westernhope Moor, Outberry Plain and Monks Moor leads towards a glorious end at Middleton-in-Teesdale.

(Parts of the Teesdale Watershed Walk can be sampled on the following walks: 6, 10, 11, 12, 14, 22, 23 & 31.)

5: THE PENNINE WATERSHED WALK

The Pennine Watershed Walk is cast rather in the same mould as the previous walk, but there is no time limit. The line of the main Pennine Watershed is imaginary and the area is rather boggy. From the A66 to the A689 at Hallbankgate the route covers 45 miles. Careful mapwork is needed to determine the line of the watershed and careful navigation is needed to walk it. This is very rough country and there are access problems, but it's a fine walk taking in all the East Fellside heights and offering tremendous views.

The low moorlands of Stainmore Common are quite rough underfoot and difficult to negotiate. Little Fell is a vast whaleback which gives way to Murton Fell and Backstone Edge on the way to Knock Fell. A fairly easy walk along the Pennine Way leads over the Dun Fells to Cross Fell. Pathless terrain continues over Melmerby Fell and Fiend's Fell to reach the Hartside Cafe. The rest of the route is hard walking over Black Fell and Cold Fell, but navigation is aided by the presence of prominent boundary fences. The hills give out at Cold Fell and a descent leads to Hallbankgate.

Parts of the Pennine Watershed Walk can be sampled on the following walks: 3, 4, 6, 7, 8, 9, 10, 11, 12, 15 & 16.)

6: RAILWAY RAMBLING

The North Pennies are not really appreciated in respect of their former railways. In Durham a number of old lines have been converted for leisure use, or at least public access has been allowed. From locations as varied as Newcastle, Sunderland or Durham, old railway trackbeds can be followed to the former steelworks town of Consett. At that point the Waskerley Way heads straight for the North Pennines. Other old lines can be added to this to offer a 25 mile route from Consett to Wearhead - from the fringe of the North Pennines to its heart.

Leave Consett by crossing the Hownes Gill Viaduct and walk along the Waskerley Way. This leads uphill to Waskerley and Parkhead. Continue along the old trackbed from Parkhead to Rookhope and reach the village by descending a long incline. Another incline leaves Rookhope and crosses Northgate Fell, descending almost to Westgate. There is an old railway trackbed which leads from Westgate to Wearhead, but it isn't available for walking. However, there are a series of riverside paths alongside the Wear which keep it in view to its terminus.

(Parts of this Railway Rambling can be sampled on the following walks: 29, 30, 31 & 32.)

CICERONE GUIDES

Cicerone publish a wide range of reliable guides to walking and climbing in Europe

FRANCE
TOUR OF MONT BLANC
CHAMONIX MONT BLANC - A Walking Guide
TOUR OF THE OISANS: GR54
WALKING THE FRENCH ALPS: GR5
THE CORSICAN HIGH LEVEL ROUTE: GR20
THE WAY OF ST JAMES: GR65
THE PYRENEAN TRAIL: GR10
TOUR OF THE QUEYRAS
ROCK CLIMBS IN THE VERDON

FRANCE / SPAIN
WALKS AND CLIMBS IN THE PYRENEES
ROCK CLIMBS IN THE PYRENEES

SPAIN
WALKS & CLIMBS IN THE PICOS DE EUROPA
WALKING IN MALLORCA
BIRDWATCHING IN MALLORCA
COSTA BLANCA CLIMBS

FRANCE / SWITZERLAND
THE JURA - Walking the High Route and Winter Ski Traverses
CHAMONIX TO ZERMATT The Walker's Haute Route

SWITZERLAND
WALKS IN THE ENGADINE
THE VALAIS - A Walking Guide
THE ALPINE PASS ROUTE

GERMANY / AUSTRIA
THE KALKALPEN TRAVERSE
KLETTERSTEIG - Scrambles
WALKING IN THE BLACK FOREST
MOUNTAIN WALKING IN AUSTRIA
WALKING IN THE SALZKAMMERGUT
KING LUDWIG WAY

ITALY
ALTA VIA - High Level Walkis in the Dolomites
VIA FERRATA - Scrambles in the Dolomites
ITALIAN ROCK - Selected Rock Climbs in Northern Italy
CLASSIC CLIMBS IN THE DOLOMITES
WALKING IN THE DOLOMITES

OTHER AREAS
THE MOUNTAINS OF GREECE - A Walker's Guide
CRETE: Off the beaten track
Treks & Climbs in the mountains of RHUM & PETRA, JORDAN
THE ATLAS MOUNTAINS

GENERAL OUTDOOR BOOKS
LANDSCAPE PHOTOGRAPHY
FIRST AID FOR HILLWALKERS
MOUNTAIN WEATHER
MOUNTAINEERING LITERATURE
THE ADVENTURE ALTERNATIVE

CANOEING
SNOWDONIA WILD WATER, SEA & SURF
WILDWATER CANOEING
CANOEIST'S GUIDE TO THE NORTH EAST

CARTOON BOOKS
ON FOOT & FINGER
ON MORE FEET & FINGERS
LAUGHS ALONG THE PENNINE WAY

Also a full range of guidebooks to walking, scrambling, ice-climbing, rock climbing, and other adventurous pursuits in Britain and abroad

Other guides are constantly being added to the Cicerone List.
Available from bookshops, outdoor equipment shops or direct (send for price list)
from CICERONE, 2 POLICE SQUARE, MILNTHORPE, CUMBRIA, LA7 7PY

CICERONE GUIDES

Cicerone publish a wide range of reliable guides to walking and climbing in Britain - and other general interest books

LAKE DISTRICT - General Books
LAKELAND VILLAGES
WORDSWORTH'S DUDDON REVISITED
THE REGATTA MEN
REFLECTIONS ON THE LAKES
OUR CUMBRIA
PETTIE
THE HIGH FELLS OF LAKELAND
CONISTON COPPER A History
LAKELAND - A taste to remember (Recipes)
THE LOST RESORT?
CHRONICLES OF MILNTHORPE
LOST LANCASHIRE
LAKE DISTRICT - Guide Books
CASTLES IN CUMBRIA
WESTMORLAND HERITAGE WALK
IN SEARCH OF WESTMORLAND
CONISTON COPPER MINES
SCRAMBLES IN THE LAKE DISTRICT
MORE SCRAMBLES IN THE LAKE DISTRICT
WINTER CLIMBS IN THE LAKE DISTRICT
WALKS IN SILVERDALE/ARNSIDE
BIRDS OF MORECAMBE BAY
THE EDEN WAY

NORTHERN ENGLAND (outside the Lakes
THE YORKSHIRE DALES A walker's guide
WALKING IN THE SOUTH PENNINES
LAUGHS ALONG THE PENNINE WAY
WALKS IN THE YORKSHIRE DALES (3 VOL)
WALKS TO YORKSHIRE WATERFALLS
NORTH YORK MOORS Walks
THE CLEVELAND WAY & MISSING LINK
DOUGLAS VALLEY WAY
THE RIBBLE WAY
WALKING NORTHERN RAILWAYS EAST
WALKING NORTHERN RAILWAYS WEST
HERITAGE TRAILS IN NW ENGLAND
BIRDWATCHING ON MERSEYSIDE
THE LANCASTER CANAL
FIELD EXCURSIONS IN NW ENGLAND
ROCK CLIMBS LANCASHIRE & NW
THE ISLE OF MAN COASTAL PATH

DERBYSHIRE & EAST MIDLANDS
WHITE PEAK WALKS - 2 Vols
HIGH PEAK WALKS
WHITE PEAK WAY
KINDER LOG
THE VIKING WAY
THE DEVIL'S MILL (Novel)
WHISTLING CLOUGH (Novel)
WALES & WEST MIDLANDS
THE RIDGES OF SNOWDONIA
HILLWALKING IN SNOWDONIA
ASCENT OF SNOWDON
WELSH WINTER CLIMBS
SNOWDONIA WHITE WATER SEA & SURF
SCRAMBLES IN SNOWDONIA
ROCK CLIMBS IN WEST MIDLANDS
THE SHROPSHIRE HILLS A Walker's Guide
SOUTH & SOUTH WEST ENGLAND
WALKS IN KENT
THE WEALDWAY & VANGUARD WAY
SOUTH DOWNS WAY & DOWNS LINK
COTSWOLD WAY
WALKING ON DARTMOOR
SOUTH WEST WAY - 2 Vol
SCOTLAND
SCRAMBLES IN LOCHABER
SCRAMBLES IN SKYE
THE ISLAND OF RHUM
CAIRNGORMS WINTER CLIMBS
WINTER CLIMBS BEN NEVIS & GLENCOE
SCOTTISH RAILWAY WALKS
TORRIDON A Walker's Guide
SKI TOURING IN SCOTLAND

THE MOUNTAINS OF ENGLAND & WALES
VOL 1 WALES
VOL 2 ENGLAND

*Also a full range of guidebooks
to walking, scrambling, ice-climbing,
rock climbing, and other adventurous
pursuits in Europe*

---

*Other guides are constantly being added to the Cicerone List.
Available from bookshops, outdoor equipment shops or direct (send for price list)
from CICERONE, 2 POLICE SQUARE, MILNTHORPE, CUMBRIA, LA7 7PY*

Designed & Printed by
Carnmor, London Road, Preston